EMPRESS OF HASTING

The first 80 years
of a family-run coach business

Stephen Dine

Edited, with historical introduction, by David Padgham

Published 2009 by Stephen Dine on behalf of
Empress Coaches Ltd.
10/11 St.Margaret's Road
ST. LEONARDS-ON-SEA
East Sussex TN37 6EH

Design and layout by Graham How and Cliff Brooker

Printed by The Berforts Group, Hastings

Pblished by Stephen Dine on behalf of Empress Coaches Ltd

Printed by Berforts Group Ltd,Hastings, East Sussex

ISBN 978-0-9564119-0-7

DY 5849, the first Dennis, at Caroline Place Stand c1934 after rebuilding with rails to support the hood over the body. For the first time the vehicle name 'The Empress' has been written on the nearside, and it may now be in the familiar later livery of maroon and cream. Owner Harry Phillips at left, Billy Hawes (customer) is holding a ticket, with Harry's wife Ethel Phillips at right, and their son Harry Edwin Phillips is seated inside with his grandmother Mrs. Whiteman.

DY 5849 Dennis, probably taken on one day in the early 1930s, at Caroline Place Stand, Hastings, opposite the "Royal Oak".

A NOTE ON NUMBERING:

Illustrations have been numbered in square brackets, for reference in the text: [23].

From 1971, after the business had been purchased by Tony Patten, fleet numbers were assigned to the coaches, the three post-war ex-Phillips vehicles being retrospectively numbered 1 to 3. Not all vehicles actually carried these numbers. A full Fleet List is given in Appendix IV, but to avoid confusion fleet numbers are not referred to in the main text. Instead the coaches are described by the registration number on the vehicle at the time of acquisition. In some cases these are not the original registrations due to the adoption of 'cherished' plates by previous owners and details of such changes are given in notes at the end of the Fleet List.

From 2000, after acquisition of the company by Stephen Dine, as explained in chapter 6, a further series of cherished number plates were gradually acquired, all with the numerals 1066 and with various combinations of letters, mostly of Irish origin. In some cases the same plates were successively used on several coaches and again details are given in Appendix IV. Where necessary to avoid ambiguity, these 1066 plates are shown in brackets in the captions after the previous numbers.

CONTENTS

Acknowledgements

Firstly to David Padgham, for drafting the book. Without his knowledge of local history and transport, the first sections of this book would not have been possible.
To Bob Cook, and Paul Green from the PSV Circle, also Nicolas King, for their valuable input and checking of data and discussions at each stage of production – and to the numerous other enthusiasts who have helped in our search for information.
To Tony Patten, who as Empress's owner for 28 years, was happy to discuss at length his memories and donated so much material that was thought to be lost – and especially for his patience and encouragement towards a young enthusiast who eventually took over the business!
To Phyllis Lapworth (née Phillips) for her memories and important verification of the facts from the early years.
To Ann Webb (née Phillips) for assistance in family queries.
To Mrs. Jean Donaldson for family history research.
To Graham How and Cliff Brooker, for professional help in design and layout.
Also Canon Keith Pound, Harold Corke, Ken and Sylvia Turner, Mike Hirst, Folkestone Reference Library and 'The Argus' newspaper.

PHOTO CREDITS
Harry Phillips: (title page), 1, 2, 3, 4, 5, 6, 8, 13, 14, 16, 17, 52, 53, 54.
Tony Patten:15, 25, 30, 33, 56, 58, 60, 63, 54, 66, 67, 72, 73, 74, 86.
David Padgham: 18, 21, 22. 23.
Paul Gainsbury: 32, 35.
Rob Crouch: 57, 68.
Bob Cook; 29, 32A, 32B, 35A, 59, 61.
Henry Clarke: 62, 65.
Colin Rowland: 11.
Dick Spiers: 12.
Frank Barson: 26.
John Short: 55.
Maidstone & District and East Kent Bus Club: 20.
Ladybird Photography: 44.
Evening Argus: 28.
Hastings Observer: 47.
Paul Green: 48B
Stephen Dine: all other photos.

David Padgham (on left) with Bob Cook, busy in research

Foreword

by David Padgham

It has been a pleasure to edit this book for Stephen Dine, whom I have known since before he passed his driving test twenty years ago, when he raided my archive of old photographs for the few relating to Empress – to which he has since added scores of others.

Empress Coaches has an unusual history when compared with other coach operators in the area. In the 1920s when the firm was founded, numerous one-man proprietors came and went within a few years, often ex-servicemen seeking to earn a precarious living and some using lodgings or accommodation addresses, from which they moved on without trace.

The Phillips family by contrast were already long established and respected in Hastings Old Town, and the venture of operating a coach was almost a sideline – they rarely advertised, and in street directories they described themselves primarily as musicians. The preceding generation had achieved fame as county cricketers; and the search for their origins has yielded a facet of local social history, the inclusion of which in a book on road transport will not, I hope, seem irrelevant to readers.

The Phillips family kept the business going throughout World War 2, right through to the 1970s. With the exception of a brief interlude, only two other families have been involved since then: Tony Patten brought his existing knowledge of the motor trade and, by hard work, expanded the fleet successfully for more than 25 years, while the past decade is a story of the enthusiasm and drive of a young man who has worked long hours to achieve his ambition, at the same time raising a happy family.

MAYOR'S PARLOUR
TOWN HALL
HASTINGS
TN34 1QR

The Right Worshipful The Mayor
Councillor Maureen Charlesworth

Tel: 01424 451751/01424 451069
Fax: 01424 451743
E-mail: hbird@hastings.gov.uk

What a magnificent milestone has been reached and what foresight local man Harry Phillips had in August 1929 when he founded the business.

The name 'Empress' is a major part of the Hastings and St Leonards landscape and many remember the pre-war excursions and mystery drives, the evacuation of local children [now of course adults] and the boom post-war seasonal trade.

I am delighted to have this opportunity to congratulate all involved with 'Empress' throughout the eighty years, both Stephen and his current team and all former employees and I am very proud to learn that you are the longest continuously running independent coach operator in the area.

Thank you again for your loyalty to our town throughout the eight decades and here's to the next eight!

Maureen Charlesworth
Mayor

Introduction

by Stephen Dine

This book has been produced to mark the occasion of eighty years continuous operation of a local coach business, which we believe may be a record in the south east of England.

As a business history it records the unusual background of the founding family, and shows how small operators were at the same time protected and yet restricted by the Road Traffic Acts in force between 1930 and 1980.

From another aspect it provides a unique photographic record of every coach ever operated during those years, with technical details in the Appendix to meet the requirements of the growing army of enthusiasts who are our "supporters". It is also presented as a mark of appreciation to our many loyal customers.

We have never professed to being a huge concern, had grand ideas about expansion, or of being a 'market leader'; we just quietly go on trying to achieve a good service for all our customers. We are aware though, that we live in an ever-changing world, where in the 21st. century it is vital to be able to adapt with the changing times.

Empress saw through the depression years of the 1930s. As the dark clouds of the second world war gathered, we continued by assisting in the evacuation of local people from Hastings, transporting the Home Guard and servicemen through the uncertain times, enjoyed the boom years of the 1950s and 60s and adapted to the gradual decline of traditional holidaymakers' visits to the seaside, from the 1980s onwards.

I make no apology that the early years of the history in Chapters 1 and 2 are written in a different style to my own, by David Padgham. With my basic facts and research, David has delved even deeper into these lost years to provide the valuable story of the Phillips family's background and the company's early years, something done with genuine first hand knowledge, as David worked in the local coach industry and knew Harry Phillips from his days working for Maidstone & District Motor Services in Hastings.

For the later years, Tony Patten and I have given you an honest, human story from a coach operator's point of view.

As we celebrate 80 years, it is important to be able to look back on all the changes, developments and the local scene that got us to still being here now. Bring on the next eighty!

This is first and foremost the history of a business, but it cannot be separated from the history of the unusually accomplished family who founded it. Where personal details are given, it is with the agreement and approval of surviving descendants.

1

2

3

4

5

Chapter 1.

The Phillips Family

There were many families by the name of Phillips in Hastings Old Town, some of them fishermen, others in building trades in mid-Victorian times. Our family can be traced back at least to 1724, but we will begin here with Richard, who was baptised on 12 March 1780 in All Saints Church and married Elizabeth, a cook, born in Fairlight. Their son William was similarly baptised in All Saints on 25 October 1807 and in due course was apprenticed as a cordwainer (leather worker). He married Harriet Suters, who is thought to have been born in Guestling; records state that they were married on 16 May 1837 - a few weeks before Queen Victoria came to the throne - in 'Surrey, at Christ Church'. Oddly, the parish is not named.

They set up home at 6 The Croft, on the opposite side of the Old Town in St. Clements parish. These were large houses of four and five storeys, built in about 1815 and very superior to what were later regarded as slums in the Bourne valley, and the couple must have had some capital. In the 1841 census they seem to have had paying guests - a young couple of independent means, no doubt adding to the family income. Between 1838 and 1860 they had ten children, of which only the first died in infancy. William's widowed mother Elizabeth later lived with them and would have helped to run the household. In 1841 William was still a shoemaker, but by 1851 he was Collector of Rates for the parish, a position of trust to which a son, James, was to succeed later.

The story now follows the third son, Henry, baptised at St. Clements on 27 December 1844 - perhaps a Christmas day arrival! Henry was apprenticed, alongside his eldest brother Albert, to a local cabinetmaker, and in 1867 was awarded a medal at a big local industrial exhibition, for a dressing table, which remained long with the family. Henry - and four of his brothers - had a great passion for cricket. Local lads played on the West Hill on summer mornings at 5.30am three times a week, before going to work. Hastings Central Cricket Ground (Priory Meadow) opened in 1865 when Henry - known to his fellow players as Harry - was only 20, but three years later he was invited to play for Sussex at Hove.

All five men soon became famous for their cricket achievements; on one occasion all playing for Hastings together. Arthur and Peter were both batsmen; James, an accountant, was the best local bat for 24 seasons, and played 64 matches for Sussex; Albert, the eldest, scored the first two centuries recorded in the district -both in one match! Henry himself was the greatest achiever: becoming a professional, kept wicket for Sussex for 24 years, taking 10 in one match in 1872, for long a record. As a bat he made 111 as ninth man against Australia in 1884, and once caught out W. G. Grace. He was offered a place on the ground staff at Lords, but

1 "Garden Lodge", 16 Edmund Road, home of the Phillips family from about 1880 for more than a century, and headquarters of the coach business for the first fifty years.

2 Harry Phillips (1891-1970) and his sister Helen, c1910.

3 Harry Phillips with his renowned long hair in ringlets, c1920.

4 Harry Phillips as an Ordinary Seaman, 1916 on H.M.S. Victory.

5 Harry's wife Ethel with their son "young" Harry and daughter Phyllis.

declined. Later he reverted to amateur; he was awarded benefit matches on his 20th and 30th anniversaries, and a century after the Australia match, Henry's grandson Harry presented his bat and a ball to the Sussex County Cricket archives.

By the time Henry was in his thirties he had become a builder and was married to Helen Seamons, two years his senior, a London girl from Bayswater - perhaps she had come to Hastings as a servant to one of the better-off families. By 1881 they were living at 'Garden Lodge', now 16 Edmund Road - built in the 1870s on a triangular plot on the corner of Githa Road **[1]**. This was the first occupied plot in this area of the newly laid out Clive Vale estate, the rest of which was now being developed by the British Land Corporation. Although Henry described himself as a builder in the census, and obviously had a steady income, he never advertised his business in local directories. Either he was actually employed by a master builder, of which there were many in this rapidly expanding town, or he was in partnership with others.

We can guess that he had personally built 'Garden Lodge' which was a substantial villa. They kept a 16-year old domestic servant, but had no children. Within a few years Helen died at Garden Lodge, aged 44, on 21 October 1886.

Henry found a new wife, Patty Priscilla Peck of Watford, the 28 year-old daughter of John Peck, a cabinet-maker. They married at Watford parish church on 19 April 1890. How he met her, we can only speculate, but it may not be coincidence that both of their fathers had been cabinetmakers. On 21 January 1891 a son Harry was born, and a year later a daughter, Helen Seamons Phillips - named in memory of Henry's first wife presumably - these were sentimental times **[2]**. Henry died on 3 July 1919, leaving substantial property, stocks and shares. Patty lived on with her two children until 28 January 1929, dying at Garden Lodge.

Harry, who survived until 1970 and is well remembered by local people as 'Old Harry', was to become the founder of Empress Coaches. By 1913 he had set up in business at home as a piano tuner and repairer. He was an accomplished musician and later played as part of a trio in the Queens Hotel until it was realised that he was also a shareholder there, upon which he was asked to leave. Perhaps in keeping with the part of musician, during the 1920s he allowed his hair to grow to shoulder length, allegedly never again cutting it **[3]**. In addition to a grand piano, instruments in the home included an organ and a Pianola. Harry also played the violin and gave lessons on it. In the grounds at 'Garden Lodge' he kept twelve hives of bees.

Harry's sister Helen was also working from home, and from 1927 to 1934 advertised in local directories as a piano teacher; however by this date she had become a resident patient at Hellingly Hospital near Hailsham in East Sussex (then the County Asylum) until her death in February 1942. While there she was encouraged to continue her music and helped at the hospital church.

On 10 April 1916 during the Great War Harry volunteered for the Royal Navy and was posted to HMS Victory in Portsmouth Dockyard (then the flagship of the Admiral Commandant) as an Ordinary Seaman **[4]** Less than four months later he was invalided out from Haslar Naval Hospital on Southampton Water with pleurisy. Later in life he was a member of the Services Rendered Club, and of the Conservative Club.

Harry resumed his old occupation of musician, and in April 1924 was married at Fairlight Church to Ethel Whiteman, youngest daughter of a well-known Rye photographer; they had a son Harry Edwin and a daughter Phyllis [5]. The latter is still living and has been of considerable help with details of the family story.
On their mother's death in 1929 Harry and Helen would have inherited the house in Edmund Road, and probably a good sum of money for the time.

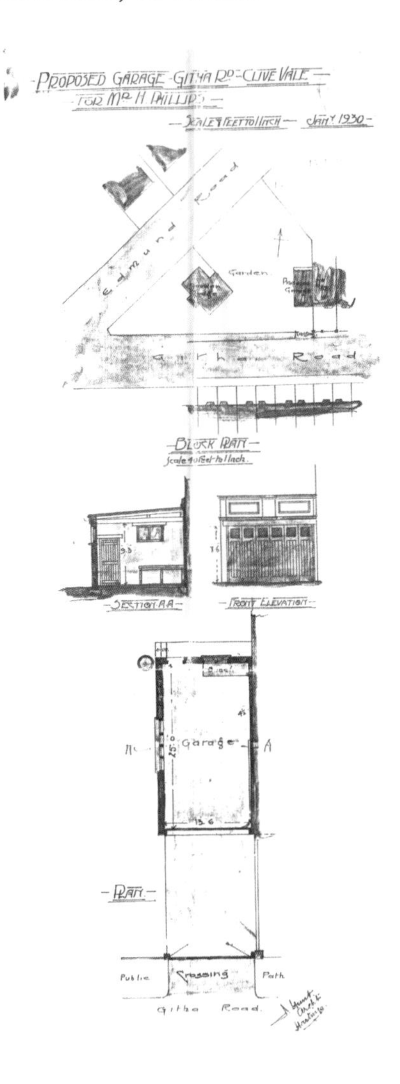

10 1930 site plan showing new garage in Githa Road.

6

8

EMPRESS COACHES

Private Hire a Speciality

Phone 162

Proprietor H. Phillips

Garden Lodge, 16 Edmund Road

Clive Vale Hastings

9

11

12

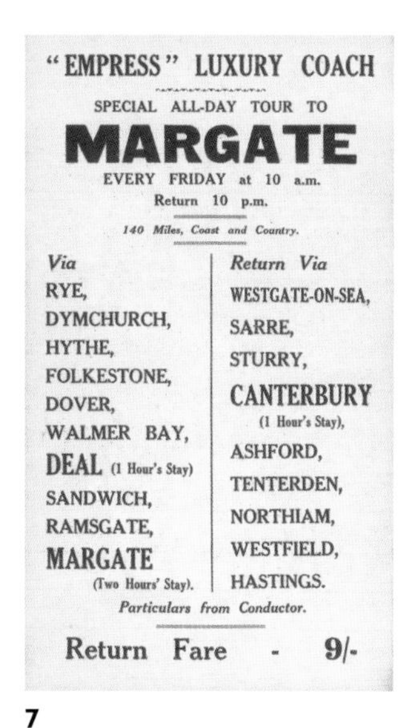

7

Chapter 2.

Early coach operations and historical developments

Like his father, Harry senior played cricket, for Hastings Ramblers, and was involved with Clive Vale Bowling Club. Within a few months of becoming head of the household, he diversified his business interests and purchased a motor coach, seemingly for the convenience of the cricket team travelling to away matches! This was a 20-seat Dennis with a canvas hood **[6]**, registered in Hastings as DY 5849 on Saturday 31 August 1929; it is described in detail in Appendix III.

No doubt Harry had taken legal advice and was aware that the impending Road Traffic Act 1930 would place tighter restrictions on newcomers to the coach industry if he delayed more than a year. Under the old system he had only to apply to the Hastings Corporation for a vehicle test and a licence plate, enabling him to operate excursions and to ply on the coach ranks on the seafront. If he planned to operate through other large towns such as Brighton he would also need their licences.

The local licence was renewed in July 1930 with plate no. 169 which had to be affixed to the rear of the coach - similar in purpose to the plates on taxis. Under the new Act this made Harry an 'established operator' and as the newly appointed Traffic Commissioners ploughed through the large volume of applications, on 26 June 1931 he was granted a Road Service Licence to operate excursions and tours - initially restricted to the tourist season between April and October. Travelling conditions in mid-winter would not of course have been pleasant in this type of vehicle. Private hires such as the cricket team were less strictly regulated and could continue, though now subject to certain rules about advertising and fares.

The earliest surviving record of a private hire estimate is from the 'Kings Head' in Battle to take a party of 20 to Brighton Races on Wed. 5 August 1931, leaving at 8.30am and arriving home at 9.40pm after various refreshment stops on the way. £5.10.0. [£5.50] was the price quoted for the 90 mile round trip, ie: 5/6d, about 27p per person, but it is not known whether or not this was accepted.

The new licence still permitted the coach to stand at Caroline Place on Hastings seafront for the sale of tickets for the excursions, the most popular being to race meetings at Brighton, Folkestone, Lewes, Lingfield, and Goodwood. On some days there were afternoon trips to the Rother Valley, followed by an evening run to a village inn such as the 'Plough' at Westfield at a fare of 1/9d (about nine pence in present coinage). Every Friday they advertised an all-day tour to Margate **[7]**, stopping on the way out at Deal and in Canterbury on the homeward trip. The fare was nine shillings [£0.45].

6 The first coach: DY 5849, Dennis 20-seater, bought in 1929. Location unknown, perhaps pre-delivery.

7 Poster advertising all-day tour to Margate in the 1930s.

8 Harry Phillips on his Swanbrook motor-cycle DY 2198, at Garden Lodge.

9 Business card for "Empress Coaches" – though only one was operated.

11 The second coach: CKF 783, Bedford WTB 26 seater, acquired in 1939, parked in London at Eccleston Bridge, Victoria Station in the 1950s.

12 CKF 783 picking up the Spiers family of Clive Vale, for evacuation in 1940.

13

14

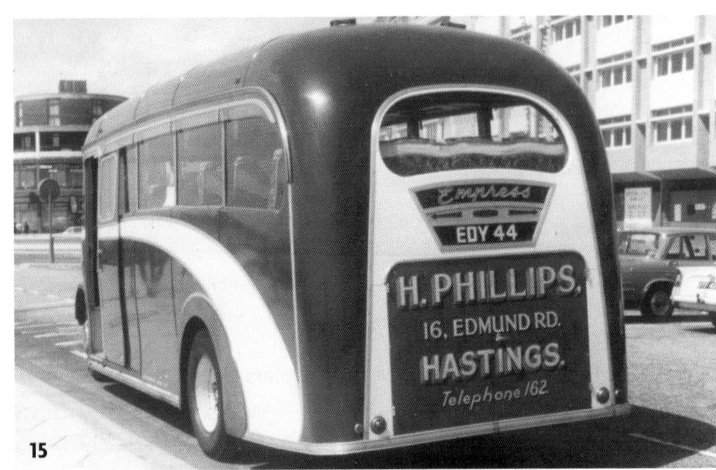

15

16

17

18

Harry would stand by the coach and sell tickets [see photo on title page] – or sometimes a Mr. Sargent stood in for him and acted as Conductor. Competition was fierce and there was good-natured rivalry with touts working for the other licensed operators, each firm keen to 'get away' with at least the minimum viable passenger loading. With only 20 seats, even a full load would bring in less than £10 on a good day, although wages were low and drivers relied on tips from the holidaymakers.

Unusually, Harry never drove his own coach, but employed a driver - whose identity is not firmly established. Harry did ride a motor-cycle **[8]**, but his reluctance to drive any other vehicle may be attributable to injury when he was a passenger in a car which, while going through Lewisham, was overturned by being caught in tram-lines. He was in hospital for some time.

Other firms who gained licences and often plied alongside Harry Phillips' coach included the major bus company 'Maidstone & District', who later took over the large family coach operators Timpsons and Skinners; and Rambler Coaches - the only one still trading today in the ownership of the original family, Rowland. The Scout Motor Co. survived until 1953 under a variety of owners, while William Gibbins' 'Queen of the Glens', F. Smith's 'Star Comfy Coaches', Jimmy Spiers' 'Village Belle' from Ore and A.E. Mogridge's 'Renown' all faded away by the outbreak of World War 2.

These small, often one-man operators usually gave names to their vehicles in this way; early photos of the Phillips' Dennis show no name painted on the sides, but by 1934 it was designated 'The Empress' - reasons for the choice are unknown, but it has been remarked in other parts of the country that 'regal' names for charabancs far out-numbered any other category. Did 'The Empress' claim to be one degree higher in the social scale than the 'Queen of the Glens'? A business card was titled 'Empress Coaches' **[9]** but it was to be several years before a second coach was added.

In January 1930 planning consent was granted for a small garage with inspection pit and petroleum store to be built on the other frontage of the triangular house plot, adjacent to 10 Githa Road **[10]**. It was enlarged in 1961 and remained in use until 1991.

A further reason for Harry to acquire a motor coach, in addition to conveying his sporting friends, was for the benefit of visitors to Hellingly Hospital - including his own relatives, as his sister was already a patient there. It was in a fairly remote location, not served by direct buses from Hastings, and Harry's daughter recalls from her early childhood, before they had the coach, how they used to take a train to Polegate, and change on to the 'Cuckoo line' as far as Hailsham, from where there was a two mile walk. It appears that the coach was made use of straight away - perhaps on a private basis by invitation, though there were fewer restrictions initially under the old licensing scheme.

On applying to renew the excursion licence for 1932 Harry was authorised to extend his season to run from March to December. He sought to add half-a-dozen new destinations, including Hellingly, which for some reason had not been listed in the initial application; but the grant published on 2 April 1932 still did not include this place. No changes were applied for in the

13 "Young" Harry's future wife May - not with the firm's vehicle, but Horace Funnell's milk van which Harry drove before passing his PSV test.

14 EDY 44, the new Bedford OB with Plaxton 29 seat body, delivered in 1950; outside the depot in Githa Road.

15 EDY 44, rear view at Breeds Place Coach Stand in July 1971, its last year of service. Tony Patten had just purchased the business.

16 EDY 44 with a party on pilgrimage to Walsingham from St. Mary Star of the Sea Church in Hastings Old Town; May Phillips is kneeling in the front row and the parish priest is in the rear.

17 CKF 783 in the 1950s on a group outing; the new driver "Tom" Thomas is second from left.

18 EDY 44 in Hastings Coach Station (now Priory Meadow shopping centre) on hire to Maidstone & District Motor Services Ltd, as one of 48 coaches despatched that evening on their London express service, a 6.30pm relief journey as far as Lewisham, on Whit-Monday, 14 May 1951. Harry Phillips, father and son, are among the crowd on the right.

1933 renewal but although it has not yet been possible to check the records for later years, it is certain that a licence was eventually obtained before the outbreak of war, and this was something of a niche market for Empress Coaches. Operations continued throughout World War II until the final run on 18 December 1983 following continued decline in passenger numbers. By 1950 and perhaps pre-war, agreement was reached with Maidstone & District Motor Services over days of operation and when bookings were few, passengers were on occasion transferred to the other firm's coach.

The service was well patronised and on occasions a relief coach was hired from another local firm, Skinners. Harry's wife Ethel would travel on the coach as a supervisor.

Just before the outbreak of war in 1939, another coach was acquired: CKF 783, a Bedford WTB built in 1937, with 26 seat rear-entrance body by Wilmotts Motors Ltd. of London W.6 **[11]**. This was new to Barker's Motors Ltd. of Wavertree, Liverpool, where the registration plate was issued, though exact details of how and when Harry Phillips bought it are uncertain; it may have been through a dealer. The original Dennis was probably not used any more; by October 1941 it was reported to be running for Mountain Transport Ltd. of London SW1.

Tourist trade vanished on the outbreak of World War 2, but a limited supply of petrol was allowed for essential work, including the hospital service. The new coach was used to evacuate local children in 1940 **[12]**, and it regularly carried the Home Guard to 'Rocklands' on the East Hill in the evenings for duty. Hop-pickers were carried during the early autumn. Two local men are known to have driven the coach at this time: Bill Shirley of 37 High Street, and Fred White, a Newsagent at 44a All Saints Street.

Petrol rationing continued for some years after the end of the war, but limited excursion work became possible in the summer of 1946. There was less competition as several firms had ceased trading, and even the larger ones were short of fuel and coaches. Austerity holidays at the seaside, which had been a restricted zone for six years, became possible; popular day trips were to Canterbury, Brighton and Dover, although there was little for tourists to see other than the castle for some years to come at this heroic bomb-stricken port.

In 1946 'young' Harry Edwin Phillips – usually known as 'Son' among family and friends – passed his PSV (Public Service Vehicle) driving test at the age of 21, and took on the regular driving duties. Driving the pre-war Bedford for the test, he recalled being sent up Old London Road and told to turn left into Richmond Street, one of the steepest hills in Hastings. Here the examiner disembarked, placed a matchbox under the rear wheel and signalled Harry to move off. Had the coach rolled back even slightly, crushing the matchbox, it would mean failure. Harry passed! In 1949 he married May Bumstead. **[13]**.

By 1949 the pre-war Bedford was in need of being supplemented by a more modern coach, but only a limited number of chassis were being released for the home market, and there was a waiting list, and little choice of body design. Harry knew exactly what he wanted - the new Bedford OB with coach body by Plaxtons of Scarborough. Neither manufacturer was allowed to deal directly with buyers at the time, but Vauxhall Motors referred him to their agent, Martin Walter Ltd. of Folkestone. Plaxtons would be delighted to do business but had been informed that all Bedford chassis had to be fitted with Duple bodies. Eventually his persistence won the day, and he was able to go to Scarborough on 1 February 1950 with 'young' Harry, who drove home his M3 Deluxe Sunshine Coach with extras including better quality seats, linoleum floor and a 'Radiomobile' wireless, all at a cost of £2012.10s.0 - more than £550 in excess of the basic Bedford/Duple model which everyone else had to be content with! **[14, 15]**. To mark this new era in his business, Harry joined a professional trade body, the Passenger Vehicle Operators' Association, at the end of March.

Registered in Hastings: EDY 44, this coach gave more than 21 years' service and is fondly remembered by many customers **[16]**. For the first time two vehicles could work together and another regular driver, 'Tom' Thomas was taken on **[17]**, usually driving the new coach and 'son' Phillips the pre-war one. Driver Tom's actual name was Clarence Stanley Thomas, and he had gained driving experience as joint proprietor of Thomas & Russell's motor garage in Middle Street, Hastings in pre-war days. He now lived at 53 Burry Road, St. Leonards-on-Sea, and his coach was a familiar sight parked overnight on the forecourt of an adjacent property by his back gate.

At times the new coach was hired by the major local operator, Maidstone & District, as an additional relief on their express service to London **[18]**. One memorable night in the 1950s there was thick fog on the way and Harry senior travelled as a pilot. At times he was having to shine a torch out on to the kerb to follow the way ahead and in Sevenoaks they unwittingly followed the kerb right into a car park!

Among the work now undertaken, in addition to the private hire and seafront excursion trade **[19]** - at its all-time post-war peak in the 1950s - was the transport of 'extras' to Camber Sands, east of Rye, Sussex for the 1958 filming of 'Dunkirk' starring John Mills, Bernard Lee and Richard Attenborough. The beach at Camber was suitable as it had similarities with its neighbour across the Channel, at Dunkirk in France.

In May 1960 a second-hand Bedford, BEN 301, was acquired, an SB3 with Duple Vega 35 seater body **[20]** replacing the pre-war CKF 783 which was sold to Crystalate Ltd. of Tonbridge, who used it as staff transport until being broken up in 1965. The garage, designed to house the original small Dennis, was now too small being only 26 feet x 13 feet, and planning consent was obtained in January 1961 to extend it to 34 x 16ft., the roof being raised at the same time **[21, 22]**. The work was carried out by local builders Spiers & Son, who, by coincidence, recalled that they had been evacuated to Welwyn Garden City in 1940 in the old WTB and that one of the boys had accidentally broken the glass in the rear passenger door.

The two Bedfords continued in use throughout the 1960s, and in some years during the winter months one of them was laid up for a repaint in the depot, leaving the other to operate the Hellingly Hospital journeys **[23]** and the occasional hire. They were augmented in September 1967 by a third Bedford, EJK 350, a 1958 model Duple Super Vega which, with 41 seats, was the largest yet owned. It came from Jackson Bros. (Palmerston Coaches) of Eastbourne, who had fitted it with a lower ratio rear axle suitable for hill work on their Beachy Head and South Downs excursions.

Phone : HASTINGS **162**

THE EMPRESS COACHES

Proprietors : H. PHILLIPS & SON

16 EDMUND ROAD -:- HASTINGS

EXCURSIONS - TOURS - PRIVATE HIRE

19

20

21

22

23

24

In June 1970 Harry Phillips senior, founder of the firm, passed away at the age of 79 after 41 years in control. His son Harry Edwin succeeded, but was still happier in the driving seat than in back-room management, and none of his children were interested in coming into the business. In little more than a year, on 1 July 1971 he sold out to Anthony W Patten, of 1 Magdalen Road, St. Leonards-on-Sea, who had previously worked as Stores Manager for the local Vauxhall/ Bedford agency, Coombs Motors. The widowed Mrs. Ethel Phillips for many years continued to accept bookings by telephone at the old address, although the office had formally moved to the new address; she lived on until November 1985, still at Garden Lodge 56 years after they had founded the business. The old garage remained in use in addition to new premises, until early 1991.

The detailed history of these decades will be told in later chapters, but briefly Tony Patten continued to trade until 5 January 1998 when he agreed to sell to a local businessman, Jan Auer. He was the principal of Broomham School, a private boarding school in Guestling, a few miles north east of Hastings, and had a few months earlier founded Blackbridge Ltd., initially to provide transport for the pupils, but with plans for expansion. In March the Blackbridge company was wound up and replaced by the old-established Empress Coaches name, which was made a limited company. At the end of March 1998 Mr. Auer appointed as his transport manager one of the young Empress employees, Stephen Dine. In December 1999 Stephen was able to purchase the business, which Mr. Auer found time-consuming to run alongside his other interests.

Stephen Dine, like the Phillips who founded the business, comes from an Old Town family and as a teenager in the early 1980s, living in Harold Road near the original Empress depot, he got to know the coach drivers **[24]**, and took on some evening and weekend cleaning work at the newer St. Margaret's Road premises. In 1986 at the age of 15 he actually purchased one of their old coaches, Bedford DHN 455C; although he was far too young to drive it, working on it was good engineering practice. Occasionally the firm hired it back for a day to meet a shortage. Encouraged by Tony Patten he trained as a mechanic and at the age of 18 in 1989 became one of the youngest holders of a PSV (Public Service Vehicle) licence in the area and could at last legally drive his own coach as well as for Empress. In the following year he left to work for Cooks Coaches of Westfield, but soon returned to 'the old firm'.

For three seasons, from 1 April 1995 until late 1997, Stephen set up his own coach business in Hastings as 'Acclaim Travel', with a single vehicle – a heavy Leyland – to gain industry experience, eventually returning to Empress a few weeks before the business was acquired by Jan Auer.

19 Business card from the 1950s.

20 BEN 301, the Bedford SB3 acquired in 1960 from a Cornish operator, at Rye on an afternoon trip.

21 BEN 301 in Githa Road at the side of "Garden Lodge", on 14 March 1971. On the right is the depot, after enlargement to hold two coaches.

22 BEN 301, rear view, taken in Githa Road on the same occasion as Fig.21 - a few months before the sale of the business to Tony Patten.

23 EDY 44 picking up at Harold Place for the Hellingly Hospital excursion, 12.15pm on Sunday 3 February 1957.

24 Stephen Dine, aged 13, with Tony Patten and driver Jim Glasgow, in Boulogne in 1984.

From the ending of the Phillips dynasty in 1970, the history of Empress Coaches moves from being a matter of documentary record to a narrative of living memory, and at this point Stephen Dine takes up the story himself.

'Big Ben' makes work a pleasure

The scene soon after the crash, showing the badly-damaged coach and car,

Chapter 3.

Tony Patten's first twenty years, 1971-1990

25 Tony Patten, who purchased the business in July 1971; an earlier portrait taken in 1959 standing beside a Rambler coach.

26 BEN 301 with its new lease of life after sale in 1971 to St. Margaret's Primary School in Crawley for use on educational trips. The driver, on the top step, is the school caretaker Frank Barson.

27 6666 AH, a Bedford SB1, the first addition to Tony Patten's fleet, in the garage at Githa Road. (left to right) Doug Sutch, Tony Patten, Brian Gain.

28 EJK 350 at the scene of the accident in Whatlington Road while on an evening "Mystery Tour" in August 1972. The Triumph collided with the almost stationary coach, bouncing off to the side of the road. The car driver later died in hospital; none of the coach passengers were seriously injured, but the vehicle was written off.

29 XBK 576, the replacement for the crashed coach, at Breeds Place Coach Stand.

30 GPC 58C, the first 36-foot long coach, too long to fit into the garage. On the way to Walsingham on 2 June 1973, with Tony Patten, May Phillips and Father Kiley.

Harry Phillips had, since founding Empress Coaches, built up a steady business; after forty-one years of operating, he passed away on 15 June 1970 at the age of 79 years. His son Harry took over the running of the Empress Coaches from his father. Always happier behind the wheel and with none of his children wishing to follow into the coach industry, just over a year after his father's passing, Harry made the decision to sell the business. On 1 July 1971 Anthony Patten (usually known as Tony), who had previously worked as stores manager for Coombs Motors, the local Vauxhall/Bedford agents, became the company's next owner **[25]**.

For the then considerable sum of £2000, he acquired the excursions and tours licences, goodwill and the three coaches; two Duple bodied Bedford SBs (BEN 301 and EJK 350) and the Plaxton Bedford OB (EDY 44) purchased new by Harry Phillips senior 21 years earlier.

The older of the SBs BEN301 was normally parked outside the garage in Githa Road, with the OB and newer SB carefully manoeuvred inside the compact building alongside each other. The only other vehicles normally in the road at this time were a lone car and a C&C Marshall truck outside No 16.

Although the business trading address and telephone number were changed to Tony's home, 1 Magdalen Road in St Leonards on Sea, with his mother Maud initially assisting by taking any telephone messages, many customers would still be calling through to Mrs. Phillips senior up at Garden Lodge, but she was happy to continue dealing with the enquiries and bookings that came through on the long established telephone number Hastings 162. There was an added advantage to this, now having two telephone numbers available to potential customers.

Tony had no dramatic ambitions for his new fleet and chose just to see how things happened, running Empress as 'business as usual'. His first trip under new ownership was on hire for another operator to Dover followed by an excursion in the 41- seater that evening, accumulating £1 in tips at the end.

As Tony recalled: "On the purchase of the business, Harry gave me a piece of exercise book paper with five customers' details written on it! Hastings Athletic Club was one and a Golf Club another. The latter came back for three trips, although Harry had not apparently been charging very much as when I billed them for something like 20 pence per mile they went mad!" On one of their trips, Tony took the club to Piltdown; he remembered it was a baking hot day, in fact so hot that when he had parked up on a grassy area he ended up opening the side flap of the coach and lying underneath the vehicle to try to keep cool.

A fleet numbering system was introduced, with the ex-Phillips 29,35 & 41 seat vehicles becoming numbers 1,2, & 3 respectively.

Empress were still running the trips to Hellingly Hospital and Tony travelled as a passenger on his first Sunday's trading to see how things operated. Although by then the trips overall never really paid for themselves, they had a loyal following of passengers on the regular Wednesday afternoon and the first Sunday of every month departures.

On private charter bookings, typical hire rates for a 41 seat coach at the time were: Windsor £27, London £22, Canterbury and Dover £18 and Brighton a respectable £14.

Until this time all previous coaches operated by the Phillips family had been petrol-engined, although there would be a switch to diesel for future purchases. The only petrol vehicles from then on to enter the fleet would be a handful of minibuses over the next two decades.

On 12 July 1971 the new Tonbridge by-pass on the A21 road from Hastings to London opened, showing a taste of the future changes that Tony would see operating coaches in his forthcoming years.

BEN 301 was sold in August 1971 to local coach dealer Ted Ive for £120 and found a new home at St Margaret's Primary School in Ifield, Crawley. After parents raised £220 to buy the coach from Ive it was appropriately named by the children "Big Ben" and was to have a new life taking classes on weekly trips and even managed a 900 mile round trip touring Snowdonia in Wales. Carefully driven by the school caretaker Frank Barson it also had occasional use as a temporary classroom if needed **[26]**.

Tony, being told some years later of BEN's adventures, seemed mildly surprised as he recalled that it had been said the coach had poor oil pressure, and when taken down to the seafront to ply its trade for local excursions it had been known for its rocker box cover to be taken off and rockers on top of the engine oiled before it departed. Mr. Barson, in a telephone interview some years ago, did recall how he thought he nearly seized the engine tackling one of the passes in Snowdon.

BEN was later reported by the PSV Circle enthusiast magazine as a static caravan re-registered and standing in woodland near Crawley in the late 1970s. It was replaced by another later diesel engined Bedford SB 41 seat Duple registered 6666 AH, purchased on 14 October 1971 for £300 from the dealer Yeates **[27]**. Tony finally had it ready for its first private hire booking exactly three months later, after spending a further £480 on it. There was an unintended slight difference in the shade of maroon that had been applied to it on repainting, almost looking more of a red - much to the displeasure of Mrs. Phillips.

Tony had a slight advantage, in that although new to the coaching game, he already knew nearly all of the coach operators locally from his days at Coombs Motors and their association with Bedford vehicles. At times he was often called upon by other operators to sub-contract work. On one occasion Tony had been on hire to Waterhouse Coaches in Polegate to help cover a contract that they had with a bank, transporting staff into and out of London during rail strikes, and it was on one of these journeys returning to Caterham in Surrey, at the last setting-down point, that a fuel line fractured on 6666 AH bringing it to a standstill. With only

one person left on board staying for moral support, Tony managed to file off the end of the broken fuel pipe, get the nut back on, and successfully tighten it to get the coach running again, although badly burning his arm on the exhaust manifold in the process - with the scars to prove it remaining some years later.

Empress still had its excursion licences and Tony made good use of them. He didn't diversify from what the Phillips family had been running as it was a good range of destinations and with the additional paperwork involved in making changes, and potential objections from other operators, he felt it was not worthwhile.

From the time when Tony took over Empress in July 1971 over seventy-seven excursions, race meetings and drives departed from the Breeds Place coach stand on Hastings seafront that year, running through until late into the season in November. Harry's fishing trips with the Clive Vale Angling Club, departing most Sundays from March until October, were a regular part of the company's activities, with places such as Eden Waters near Edenbridge, Snailham, Blackwall, Newenden, East Guldeford, Winchelsea, Bodiam and Wallers Haven near Eastbourne part of the regular calendar.

The locally well-known Bedford OB Plaxton, EDY 44 continued in service until the end of the 1971 season, and was withdrawn when its fitness certificate was due on 9 January 1972 after a creditable twenty-two years service to the company. It found a new home with the Pestalozzi Children's Village in nearby Sedlescombe, later moving on to Uckfield Scouts. Last reported still requiring restoration with Mole Valley Transport in Surrey sometime in the 1980s, it was sold on again, its final fate unknown.

A new Sunday church contract began on 4 June 1972 for the Salvation Army in St Andrews Square in Hastings, joined later in the year by the nearby Robertson Street United Reformed Church, which ran neatly together using one coach until the 1990s.

Afternoon and evening drives remained popular for the 1972 season, beginning on the spring bank holiday at the end of May, with takings for a coach normally averaging out at anything from £6 up to sometimes nearly £12 overall for the vehicle on a good loading, if touting for customers passing the coach stand had been brisk. For example a return fare for a day trip to Canterbury would be 65 pence per head.

With over forty departures for the drives alone already undertaken, this was all shattered on 22 August 1972 when one of the coaches was involved in a serious accident. Harry Phillips had set off on an evening departure from the Hastings seafront coach stand in the 41 seater on a mystery drive through the local countryside. After a brief stop outside Battle Abbey, Harry then made his way up the High Street and out onto Whatlington Road. Mystery drives were generally operated at a leisurely pace, and travelling through the lane at 15 to 20 mph Harry could see a Triumph car coming towards him at speed and had pulled virtually to a standstill into the hedge, knowing that an impact was inevitable.

The car collided with the front offside of the coach, hitting it so hard that it actually bounced off the vehicle. As a witness on the coach said, the car came "like a bolt out of the blue". Fortunately none of the passengers had sustained serious injuries in the chaos that followed,

although Harry had a leg caught by the coach's brake pedal and later needed stitches. He recalled how it was touch and go whether the trip was run at all that night due to a low loading of passengers.

A fleet of three ambulances from Battle and Bexhill rushed to the scene, ferrying the injured to the Royal East Sussex Hospital in Hastings. Harry tried to help the motorist although he was trapped in the car, so he used the coach's fire extinguisher instead as smoke was coming from the engine. The driver of the car later died in hospital **[28]**. This is the only major accident on record during eighty years of operations.

All the immediate seafront departures were cancelled, and to help out in what was the busiest time of year Monks Coaches of Staplecross assisted with a vehicle to cover some of the existing commitments.

The coach, EJK 350 was completely written off, with the offside front of the chassis badly twisted, although Tony and Harry did later salvage a few parts and the interior seats, which, with repairs were fitted into 6666 AH as they were in good condition. Ten days later another 41 seat Bedford Duple (XBK 576) had been purchased from Waterhouse coaches in Polegate to replace the former Phillips' Bedford **[29]**.

In the early days Tony never really touted for work, although one customer that did come on board was the Guardianship Society, who had been previously using two local Ive Drive minibuses to transport their ladies on a daily basis to a Community Hall. With some persuasion and the promises of a better, more reliable service using one larger coach, the new contract began in September 1972 and ran on until July 1992. *(See Sylvia Turner's memories, Appendix 1).*

Other customers that year included SAGA, Hastings Corps of Drums, Kenilworth Mission, The Grove & Priory Road Schools, Mount Pleasant Hospital, 'The Dripping Well' and the 'First In, Last Out' public houses. Sub-contract work was still undertaken for other operators during the year, such as Alex Henshaw of Rye, Warrens in Ticehurst, Renown from Bexhill, Cooks of Westfield and local companies such as Rambler and Hastings Coachways.

The first 36-foot-long coach came in May 1973, in the shape of a 52 seat Plaxton-bodied Bedford VAL twin-steer dating from 1965 (GPC 58C) **[30]**; it also had the dubious honour of being the first member of the fleet to be too long to fit into the Githa Road garage with the doors shut. It could be driven in forwards for maintenance without making contact with the garage roof due to the small 16-inch wheels giving the coach a low enough overall height, although the patience of the local neighbours was tested when a major engine overhaul was undertaken, which of course had to be done with the garage doors left open. The noise created from trying to remove the liners from its Leyland engine that went on unexpectedly into the night did not go down too well due to the sound echoing around the street.

That season from May onwards the private hire bookings were becoming quite busy so excursion work from the coach stand was not playing such a large role as previously, although later from August into September some were undertaken.

Tony considered the early 1970s his boom years. On the regular drives a tea stop destination favourite that stayed in his memory was Wannock Gardens, near Polegate. Inside was Fred's miniature village and greenhouses containing plants that actually had real bananas growing from them. When arriving at this destination Tony made a regular joke, telling the passengers to look out inside for the Water Otter. For those that found it, it was indeed a Water 'otter - a large water tank with a kettle inside as labelled!

It was not unusual for the weekend evening drives to go on quite late into the year, sometimes being nearly dark before even setting off. On one tour, Tony was stopped driving up Rye Hill by a local policeman for not having his interior lights on. Although this has always been a requirement of PSV regulations, Tony explained light-heartedly that it was a mystery drive after all - the policeman did eventually let him go, but was not amused.

Race meetings were still popular, including destinations such as Goodwood, Ascot, Wye, Epsom, Plumpton, Folkestone and Brighton **[31]**.

In July 1973 a coach (usually XBK 576 or 6666 AH) was loaned to the local council for their school contract duties in the Hastings area, as they were experiencing problems with their own bus. This became a more regular arrangement, through the following year and into the 1975 season before a new bus was finally delivered to them. Its regular driver was John Heath, who was also happy to help out with occasional private hire work at Empress, eventually taking up a regular position at Empress when the school bus was finally sold in the 1990s.

October 1973 brought Empress's first minibus into the fleet, a 1969 Ford transit 12-seater (NDK 653G) purchased from Graham's Coaches of Rye, a taste of things to come, and pointing the way to the smaller vehicles in the future line-up. Not painted into fleet livery, it retained Graham's distinctive blue colours.

That same month, on an international scale, the Middle East stopped fuel exports to the western nations including the United Kingdom, causing what became the oil crisis. Fuel prices quadrupled, and even after the embargo ended a year later oil prices remained higher than previously. Tony had traded in profit until this point, although as inflation went up it took a long time after this to recover from the soaring operating costs.

In the following February a rare model purchased was a 1965 Bedford VAS with Plaxton 33 seat coachwork (DHN 455C), a second vehicle from Waterhouse Coaches in Polegate **[32]**. This coach was one of only six of its type to have its chassis cut and lengthened when new by chassis specialist Don Everall, before being bodied by Plaxton in Scarborough to accommodate 33 seats instead of the normal 29-seat layout. A popular size in the fleet, it enjoyed a long stay, remaining in service until 1987.

By 1975 the fleet had grown to five vehicles; although there was space outside Githa Road garage as well as inside, some vehicles were kept on waste ground behind residential houses in nearby Canute Road. On one occasion Tony went to collect the Bedford VAL and noticed one of its front wheels had sunk into the ground. It soon became apparent that an old long forgotten well had collapsed beneath it. Even though the coach's second front axle held the vehicle up it was with some difficulty that the coach was removed from its parking place.

Tony had been working well with another local operator, Pandora Holidays Ltd., owned by Mike Tilyard, and based in a rented garage at 10-11 St Margaret's Road, St Leonards-on-Sea,

Empress Coaches

A. W. PATTEN

1 MAGDALEN ROAD, ST. LEONARDS . Hastings 430621
TN37 6EG 437162

PRIVATE HIRE ∴ ENQUIRIES WELCOME
EXCURSIONS AND TOURS

Race Meetings at:—

Brighton . Plumpton . Lingfield . Wye . Folkestone

Visitors to Hellingly Hospital every Wednesday afternoon at 12.55

All the above start from Hastings Sea Front Coach Stand

31

32

33

34

35

36

31 Publicity card from the 1970s.

32 DHN 455C, the rare lengthened Bedford VAS with 33 seat Plaxton body; Vince Lavender driving.

33 KRL 905L, a Bedford NJM with 41 seater Duple body, at Breeds Place coach stand in 1976 with Tony Patten endeavouring to sell excursion tickets.

34 Line-up at St. Margarets Road Depot in 1980: Bedfords KNK 357G, DHN 455C, VAL 965L.

35 VAL 965L, Bedford YRT with 53 seat Plaxton body, working on Debenham's Free Shopping service in the early 1980s, Tony Patten driving.

36 DHN 455C in 1986 with driver John Collier, leaving the Depot, alongside JHC 178Y, a Bedford PJK 29 seater.

and on the 1st July 1975 Tony and Mike unofficially amalgamated their operations. Mike had purchased Pandora back in 1973 from local businessman George Hirst for whom Mike had previously driven.

Pandora operated a mixture of extended tours, private hire, schools and factory contract work so with the two companies operating different types of business and both being busy, it was felt that 'joining forces' seemed to make sense. Pandora was one of the trading names chosen by George Hirst for his Hastings Coachways Ltd. operation originally incorporated in March 1961. Moving with the times, many new coaches were operated specialising in UK and continental tours; the business was a market leader in its day. George had originally operated taxis in St Leonards and was reputed to be the first man in the town to have radio-controlled cabs as Radio Cartax. In 1958 he bought the first minicoach in the district. George's son Mike Hirst and daughter-in-law Kathi later founded the very successful Travel Time in Robertson Street, Hastings, in 1976.

After Empress and Pandora had worked together that season the association proved unsuccessful, and following a meeting on 15 December both parties agreed to dissolve the partnership, finally ceasing on 31 December 1975, Tony taking his vehicles that were parked at Pandora's depot back to his Githa Road garage the following day. In the following months Tony was in the difficult position of having to tout again for his old customers as many were now calling through on Pandora's telephone number.

Tony's first new purchase came in April 1976, a Bedford CF 12-seat minibus with Perkins diesel engine and conversion by Robin Hood (MPE 777P), originally ordered by Mike Tilyard along with a Duple-bodied Bedford PJK. While Pandora did take delivery of the coach, they had cancelled the order for the smaller vehicle. Tony was approached by the sales representative from Robin Hood conversions and decided to have the mini-bus himself.

From 1 April 1977 Pandora needed three additional large vehicles for the new pensioners' bus service contract that had been successfully awarded to them by the local council, having previously been operated by Maidstone & District. Mike decided to purchase Bedford VAL twin steers, being within budget, as the council would not offer the contract for a long enough period to invest in more suitable stock. The choice of vehicle proved unsuitable for the hilly Hastings area. Tony was relining the rear brakes at least once a month on his own VAL, as well as regular brake adjustments all round in between this, just running on private hire work only, so the choice of VALs for the local bus routes proved to be the downfall of the pensioners' service. A year later Pandora lost the contract, which was resumed by Maidstone & District.

Tony used his VAL in part-exchange for the new Bedford CF minibus, although the latter's stay was not for long; proving a costly vehicle to run, it was replaced the following year by a new petrol-engined Ford transit registered RDY 512S.

Alterations to the height of the doors were needed at Githa Road in July 1976 as it was discovered on purchasing a 41-seat Bedford Duple Vega 31 (KRL 905L) **[33]** that it would not go inside. This time, as the roof of the garage had fortunately already been raised some fifteen years earlier, it was the runners and sliding doors only that required additional height, so with

Harry's carpentry skills this problem was overcome.
A sign of the changing social times in 1977 was the Police contacting all local coach operators including Empress, to advise them not to take bookings for any Manchester United Supporters Clubs for a particular forthcoming football match on Sat. 7 May due to predicted trouble.
After being approached by George Hirst, Tony decided to purchase the former Pandora depot for his new main operating base in 1978, a few months after Pandora had ceased trading during June of that year, their licences being taken over by Waterhouse Coaches in Polegate **[34]**. George eventually enjoyed a long retirement after assisting in his family's travel agency business Travel Time, before passing away on 22 August 2007 in his 101st. year.
Even with a good maintenance programme, the operation of coaches, indeed any commercial vehicles, has always had an unpredictability because of unforeseen problems. One occasion that Tony remembered without affection was of a call from Harry when on tour to Walsingham in Norfolk. One of the Bedfords developed a problem with a jockey pulley bearing driving the alternator on the engine; although Harry was confident he could make it to the final destination, immediate attention was required. Initially the coach was booked in with the local Bedford agents for repair in nearby Norwich, but on the following day on an excursion the fault developed again. Frustrated by the situation, Tony left Hastings in his Vauxhall Cavalier car with more parts at 7.0pm that weekday evening and drove as fast as he could, mainly on what were A roads, arriving there at 10.30, a distance of over 140 miles. After making the necessary repairs to his own satisfaction - in the dark by torch light - he then turned around and drove home.
By the start of the 1978 season the fleet now stood at four vehicles, two coaches and two 12-seat mini buses. By this time, with the move of most of the fleet activity from Githa Road to the St Margaret's Road site, Mrs. Phillips had now retired from day to day assistance.
On the 15 June 1978 a new East Sussex County Council school contract commenced with one of the minibuses to Glyne Gap School in Bexhill, something that had previously been covered on a few occasions on hire to Pandora Holidays, who previously held the contract but had just ceased trading. This became a long-lasting association with the school that thirty years on is still an important part of the company's business and now requires four dedicated vehicles.
The following year Empress's fleet was back up to five vehicles with an even mix of regular contact work and private hire bookings keeping the fleet busy for most of the year. A popular evening venue throughout the 1970s and 1980s was Kings Country Club in Eastbourne, where on occasions big acts of the time were drawn in, including Showaddywaddy, Peters & Lee and the Baron Knights, to name a few.
Towards the end of 1979 excursions were operated on Boxing Day to take holiday-makers staying at the Queens Hotel and Randolph Hotel out for mystery drives whilst enjoying their Christmas breaks in Hastings, with the Hellingly Hospital service also running that day.
By the beginning of the 1980s the seafront excursion trade from Breeds Place coach stand had now really become part of local history, although Tony did have the 53-seater (VAL 965L) parked there over the Easter Bank Holiday 1980 to gauge potential business for some pre-booked excursions.

PARTIES FROM

12 SEATER MINI BUS CATERED FOR

RING (0424) 430621

FOR YOUR QUOTATION

Empress Coaches

13 BEDFORD ROAD
HASTINGS
EAST SUSSEX
TN35 5JA
HASTINGS (0424) 430621

Business card. c1980

A new livery of white with red and orange was adopted instead of the original maroon and ivory on the acquisition in November 1980 of a new Bedford CF 16-seat minibus (AKT 949V), this time with the Opel diesel engine. The vehicle had previously been the Dormobile Conversions demonstrator in these colours. Gradually all future purchases were to receive the new colours, with DHN 455C, by now the oldest of the fleet at 21 years of age, receiving the new livery in January 1986, and the lone VAL 965L being the last of the original liveried coaches finally sold on in the February.

It was also in late 1980 that the local department store Debenhams hired Empress for the first time for their shoppers' free bus over the Christmas and New Year holidays. Adverts promoting the service were published in the "Hastings Observer", with two separate routes using the 12 and 16-seat vehicles. It was certainly popular as it was provided again on Good Friday 1981, using the 53 and 33-seat coaches and again on Easter Monday with the mini-buses. It was repeated for the 1982 and 1983 seasons **[35]**.

The downturn in the local coach stand work in the late 1970s and early 1980s was partly compensated by a growing market for foreign students visiting the town. Early customers were language schools such as STS, HELC (Hastings English Language Centre) and Embassy, with popular destinations being Canterbury, London, Brighton as well as local events such as Arlington stock car-racing and country pubs; fortunately the student market flourished locally with excursions and transfers in the forthcoming years.

No booking had ever been too small, and on 30 October 1981 a new contract began every Friday lunchtime to take staff from Sussmans shirt factory in Parker Road into the town centre to drop them there so that staff could collect their wages. This ran for a number of years.

Empress's diverse selection of customers for the 1982 season included organisations such as The Friendly Hand Club, Helenswood School, All Souls Church in Clive Vale, Sandrock Hall on the Ridge, Osborne House, The Blind Centre and Marlborough Hotel, Warrior Square. Unusually, the fleet this year consisted of one of every popular size available: 12, 16, 29, 33, 41 and 53 seats.

One now largely forgotten trend in which Tony was active throughout most of this decade was his passion for the CB (Citizens' Band) radio craze. Before the advent of mobile phones, Tony was able to have a CB radio operational in his service van when away from the office or depot, and to be in contact with his secretary Mrs. Pat Barnett in the office at Tony's home in Bedford Road, which proved advantageous. The answering of immediate queries, which usually led to business, and assisting when other operators were in trouble, speeded up the response time. The radios did also prove popular for being stolen from vehicles, and after the third occasion of this happening to Tony he finally gave up and went on the new mobile phones that were just appearing. They were big things with aerials about six inches long, as Tony recalled, 'ideal for jabbing oneself in the ear'! So finally having true mobile contact was a great step forward if a bit laborious to start with.

The market was gradually moving towards smaller groups for Empress even back in the 1980s, when one date from the 1983 booking diary showed that on 20 August no less than five private

32A

32B

35A

32C

35B

hire bookings all requested the 29-seat size vehicle. In 1983 another new factory workers contract began using a 16-seat minibus to Buss Farm-Fresh Foods on the Ponswood estate, running on into the 1990s.

The regular scheduled excursions to Hellingly Hospital near Hailsham finally ceased on 18 December 1983, due mainly to diminishing passenger numbers, after more than fifty years' continuous operation.

The 1980s saw more purchases of mainly smaller types of vehicles within the fleet. A new Bedford PJK with Duple 29-seat coachwork (JHC 178Y) **[36]** was added to the fleet in early January 1983, and a coach-built 16-seat Ford Transit (B175 LMY) the following year. These types of vehicle formed the backbone of the fleet at this time, with other second-hand examples joining the fleet.

Mrs. Ethel Phillips, widow of Harry senior, passed away in November 1985; she had still been living at 16 Edmund Road in Clive Vale where she and her late husband had founded their coach business 56 years before.

By the middle of the 1986 season Tony was now again running a total of six vehicles, the largest amount that he was to operate. A large customer that year was the Bathing Pool Holiday Camp, situated along the far end of St Leonards seafront in Sea Road. A meeting had been held with a Mr. Wright at the Bathing Pool in February to discuss the year's programme, beginning with a large selection of mainly half-day drives departing every week throughout the season from early May until the middle of October. These trips proved very popular with holidaymakers, so the decision to finally close the camp towards the end of that year was indeed sad news.

Other customers in 1986 included Exchange Travel, HELC and the Shoreditch Hotel. 1987 continued with a pattern of contract and private hire work. With the larger size of coach not always featuring within the fleet due either to the time of year or customer demand, the line-up in the early part of 1988 was a mix of two 29-seat and two 16-seat vehicles, although in September Empress's first ever heavy-weight coach arrived – NKM 133, a Leyland Leopard with Plaxton Supreme 53-seat coach work. Most recently with Shamrock & Rambler in Bournemouth, it had been new to Midland Red in Birmingham ten years earlier, and had been used extensively on charter to the City of Birmingham Symphony Orchestra. Another unusual purchase in October 1989 was a Bristol LHS 35-seater with an early version of Plaxton Supreme coachwork (JLN 237N), again a departure from the normal loyalty to Bedfords.

In 1989 Pat Barnett retired from her secretarial work in the office, and the following year Tony's wife Judy took up the role, transferring the day-to-day telephones from their home in Bedford Road to the more central St Margaret's Road depot.

32A DHN 455C outside Githa Road depot.

32B EDY 44 pictured after disposal from Uckfield Scouts. c1977

35A Brief encounter: KRL 905L soon to be sold, (on left) with VAL 965L, just acquired. February 1980 in 'new' St Margaret's Road depot.

32C DHN 455C Debenhams shoppers' free bus. Robertson Street, Hastings. December 1980.

35B Stephen Dine (15) at St Margaret's Road Depot, 21.6.1986.

37A

37B

37C

37D

37E

37F

Chapter 4:

The 1990s - new decade, diverse business.

37A St. Margaret's Road Depot in late 1991.

37B NKM 133 with A843 XFW following. Afternoon drive with guests at the Adelphi Hotel, Warrior Square, St Leonards. October 1991. Sid Lovell driving.

37C NKM 133 & 200 FXM, (Fleet Nos 31 & 38) at Tenterden Sports Centre, Feb 1995

37D The Hastings "round the town" tour bus passes both Omnis & Ford Transit B175 LMY, waiting to collect passengers from Hastings Station. August 1993

37E B157 FWJ at Ditchling Beacon, Nr Brighton. 3.1.1993

37F Empress drivers at work! L to R Stephen Dine, Harry Phillips and Peter Pragnell. Combe Haven Holiday Park, St Leonards. August 1993

In the 1990s one popular request from customers as a different destination to visit was the Eurotunnel Exhibition Centre, situated alongside the M20 Motorway at Cheriton close to Folkestone in Kent. First opening in the September of 1988, with the public's interest in Great Britain finally becoming linked with France via tunnels underneath the English Channel, it became a favourite venue. By April 1992 over one million visitors had passed through its doors. Attractions included a full-scale mock up of a shuttle interior complete with two cars, a working thirty-metre long model railway of what the completed system would look like, and a mock up of a tunnel-boring machine.

Outside there was a twenty-one metre high viewing tower over the working site, and later the 5.36 metre diameter tunnel-boring machine, that had completed the landward service tunnel from nearby Shakespeare Cliff to Holywell Combe in 1989 was put on display next to the main building overlooking the motorway. Well-remembered by many a motorist using the M20 for some years afterwards, it later became the first tunnelling machine to be sold on the then novel eBay website fetching £39,999. Its sister machine held the record for the longest tunnel drive on a run of twenty-two kilometres between December 1987 and October 1990.

Also at this time, Tony was approached by the East Sussex County Council to see if he could provide wheelchair-accessible transport for the runs to Glyne Gap special school. The new vehicles proposed would be a complete departure from the standard-style vehicles operated. Until then those children that travelled to school requiring the use of a wheelchair had to be physically lifted on and off the vehicle, which was not an ideal situation.

After looking in the market place, three types of vehicle were identified as being suitable, low-floor access being the main requirement; the short list was for a Renault Master, Talbot Tri-axle, or the CVE Omni. Contact was made with City Vehicle Engineering Ltd (CVE) of Shildon, Co Durham, towards the end of May 1990, as their vehicle the Omni, after evaluation by Tony, was considered the best choice. It offered the highest seating and wheelchair capacity, for example 21 seats, or six seats plus six wheelchair spaces possible, with access from the rear of the vehicle by means of lowering rear air-suspension and a shallow pull-out ramp.

Tony verbally placed an order with Mr. John Marsden at CVE on the 3 July 1990 for two vehicles at a cost of £31,615 each, although Mr. Marsden offered a discount to £30,000 each if the order was confirmed in writing within seven days, which of course it was. This was not an inconsiderable sum of money in 1990 for a small operator.

Various options were offered on specification at the time, although Tony chose the recently changed standard engine choice of a Perkins 3.0 Diesel unit, even though CVE still offered

the original somewhat underpowered Land-Rover 2.5 engine if preferred. The vehicles proved very popular, and were certainly eye-catching, as there was nothing else in the local area like them. Apart from regular schools contracts the Omnis did undertake various other types of private hire bookings, some for customers requiring wheelchair accessibility instead of a full seating capacity. Airport and dockside transfers were not uncommon, with one vehicle even undertaking a Shearings Coach Holidays feeder from Worthing to Dover Docks. Probably the furthest these town and rural type vehicles travelled was on a student transfer down to Torquay in Devon and back in a day! Customers in 1990 included Penland Wood Residents Association, Adelphi Hotel and Clive Richardson Coach tours.

By early 1991 the Githa Road garage was finally vacated after more than sixty years' use. The St. Margaret's Road site had by now become the main depot due to its larger and more convenient central location **[37]**. It was increasingly difficult at times to get minibuses in and out of the old garage because of inconsiderately parked cars outside, and it was virtually impossible to manoeuvre a coach in or out at all.

Ford Transit JEC 407T was withdrawn, and had been scrapped there the previous year, on site. Its body was taken away on 13 October, and with the arrival of the new Omnis, AKT 949V and 200 FXM had been moved up to Githa Road on 25 October pending eventual disposal, the former departing in the March of the following year, finding a new home locally with the Kenilworth Mission. Harry Phillips later sold off the garage privately; it still stands today (2009), basically the same but with alterations to the front doors.

Tony's long-standing regular contract with the Guardianship Society (see Appendix 1), or 'The Girls' as they were more well known amongst the drivers finally ceased at the end of July 1992 due to cutbacks within the organisation which brought to an end a twenty-year relationship.

The pattern of work operating throughout the 1990s continued without much change, generally formed by a backbone of contract and schools work with a good mix of private hire bookings that would keep the fleet especially busy between May and September annually. Customers included Vinehall School, Charlton Athletic Supporters' Club, English For You, Charters Ancaster School, Hurst Court on the Ridge and King Offa School in Bexhill.

In conjunction with the East Sussex County Council, from 13 March 1995 both Omnis were extensively used on new mobility-link bus services in the Hastings and Bexhill area, linking with the then new Conquest Hospital in Hastings. On service 303 one journey each way M-F between Little Common and the Conquest Hospital via Harley Shute was already being worked by Bexhill Community Bus and Empress now provided several additional journeys. New services 330-334 also began from this date, each operating one day a week M-F, between Hastings Town Hall and the Conquest Hospital via different routes (for details see Appendix 2).

A third late OBC Omni, J996 MKM was purchased second-hand in July 1995 to assist the other two vehicles - due to the continuous punishment of regular schools and service work, frequent hub maintenance was required to keep them on the road. This proved to be a weakness in design, and probably the largest purchaser of the Omni, Kent County Council (KCC) assisted Tony in many of the major repairs on his vehicles within their workshops.

There were other difficulties as City Vehicle Engineering had run into financial problems, eventually being taken over and returning to the market as OBC Omni before again running into trouble, finally emerging as FTL Omni. In fact KCC was so unimpressed by some weaknesses in design of the Omnis' hubs and gearboxes that their workshops in Aylesford re-designed and engineered them for their own fleet, also fitting six speed Quaiffe gearboxes in place of the original four speed ZF types to minimize the operational problems. Empress's third Omni, a former KCC vehicle, had already been treated to these modifications.

The Bexhill to Hastings part of the mobility link services (303) became popular, but from 6 October 1996 this tender passed entirely to Renown who also took over the Bexhill Community Bus working. The unusual timetable of the Hastings town part of the second route (ie: a different area of town covered each day over the five weekdays operated) meant that takings on this were small and, combined with the lack of passengers from the dial-a-ride advertised part of the service a decision by the ESCC to finish services from the same date was regretfully made, with the exception of the Tuesday only 331 which continued until 23 June 1998. Later in that year some similar operations resumed – see the next chapter.

38

40

wu
CONQUEST HOSPITAL
Empress
Empress of Hastings
F486 XON
39

Empress
39A

Chapter 5:

The Blackbridge Years, 1998-99

By 1997 Tony was beginning to think about retirement and looking to find a suitable buyer for the business, and on 5 January 1998 he made the decision after 28 years to sell Empress Coaches to Mr. Jan Auer, a local businessman **[38]** Jan (pronounced Yan) had originally founded Blackbridge Ltd. in October 1997 as the transport side of Broomham School in Guestling, which he also owned. On learning of Tony's planned retirement he made contact, as Jan was keen to take over a well-established business. Three weeks afterwards, on 26 January 1998 Blackbridge Ltd was renamed Empress Coaches Limited, a company for the first time.

The former Blackbridge fleet, consisting of an ex-Premier-Albanian Coaches Leyland Tiger, two Ford transit minibuses and former 'Empress' Bedford PJK, joined the Empress fleet, bringing the total strength up to 11 vehicles. Tony had first started using fleet numbers for the coaches on purchasing Empress in 1971 and by the end of 1997 the then current number was 44. There was some discussion with the merging of vehicles for numbering to start again as Blackbridge's Bedford and Leyland were already numbered 01 & 02 respectively, although with some persuasion by the Empress staff the original system was retained with the Leyland becoming 45 and the Ford Transit minibuses 46 and 47, with the former Empress Bedford re-joining the fleet under its original number 39 (see Appendix 4 for full Empress fleet list).

After a somewhat difficult start to the year, Jan appointed me as transport manager at the end of March 1998. As well as our existing contract work and private hire commitments, we inherited Broomham School's two country routes, previously operated by Blackbridge, which now became a part of our business, as well as additional private hire work generated from the school itself and the Tuesday working on service 331 and EC1.

At an early stage I was keen to reintroduce an updated version of the former fleet livery of Maroon and Ivory to replace the orange red and white colours that by now had become slightly outdated. There were two reasons for this - firstly it made sense to re-awaken people in the local area to the fact that we were still trading (albeit under new ownership); also I liked the old colours! The new livery was applied to most of the fleet that summer. We adorned the sides of the vehicles with bold large vinyl lettering stating Empress of Hastings, using the new style of script chosen for our new letterheads by Mrs. Betty Keen, a member of Jan's staff. The reason for the new name was my personal awareness that potential customers may spot a coach driving past, but it is rare for them to have a pen and paper to hand to write a phone number down quickly if a future hire is of interest. By catching your name and where you are from, a simple look in the phone book will get you the contact details. Having said this, I

38 Jan Auer, the fourth owner of the business, in his office at St. Margaret's Road in 1998.

39 F486 XON, a Freight Rover 16 seater, at Hastings Station Approach on service 335 which was operated under County Council tender from Sept. 1998. The passing pedestrian is the late Cllr. David Thornton, one-time Mayor of Hastings.

39A Winter conditions on the 'schools' run, LIB 1066. Driver Philippe Bedford with bus escort Rose Dine. 2006

40 Stephen Dine with Richard Attenborough, during the filming of "Grey Owl" in Milward Road, Hastings in June 1998.

always made sure to have full contact details on the rear end of the vehicle, just in case! Jan was easy-going about the ideas. For the first time in twelve years the fleet was re-appearing in its original colours.

An early decision was to cease the commercially run EC1 bus service that ran twice daily to the Ponswood Industrial Estate. Originally the service had been operated as a private works contract for Buss Farm-Fresh Foods in Drury Lane on the estate, becoming a registered service when the contract came to an end. It was well used at the time; it was sadly withdrawn after 22 June 1998 on the closure of Phillips, a local large employer for which the service had been mainly run to serve its staff.

On 28 September 1998 a new five-times daily service funded by the ESCC began. Numbered 335, it ran between the Conquest Hospital and the town centre, linking in Hastings Station and minor roads that the larger service buses did not use **[39]**.

In addition to the 335 service, one journey each way was resumed on service 303 in the early weekday evenings, in addition to the service still being worked by Renown. To begin with it ran from Devonshire Road, Bexhill, to the Conquest Hospital via Mount Idol View in Sidley. It was extended on 19 Jan. 1999 to begin and terminate at Little Common. Anticipating future developments, to complete the story of bus operations, by June 2002 the last westbound journey was extended back to start from Helenswood Upper and Lower Schools to cater for late finishing students, but by November of that year Empress operations again ceased, leaving Renown to operate.

The 335 service was rerouted by the ESCC and merged with Coastal Coaches 346 Hastings and Pett service by July 2000, with Empress running on weekdays only between our schools commitments. In October 2003 it was renumbered 347. The Empress contribution ceased after 20 August 2004, leaving Coastal to work the full timetable. This was the final operation of bus services by Empress to date. Full details of the services are listed in Appendix 2.

1998 was also a year for new types of vehicles entering the fleet; it was around April that the Leyland Tiger (CBM 12X) acquired with the purchase of the business by Jan departed after only a few months stay.

This was eventually replaced by a 1984 DAF SB2300 (LIL 5292) with Plaxton Paramount coachwork, another unusual departure from previous purchases as it was rear-engined so its large underfloor luggage capacity came in very useful. The first purchase after the two fleets were combined was of a Toyota Caetano Optimo 21-seat mini-coach (K885 BRW). This stylish vehicle had the drive-and-ride quality of a private car, and the high point of its stay in the fleet was in June 1998 when hired by film company Beaver Productions, to transport the Director of filming Lord (Richard) Attenborough and his immediate team to and from location in Milward Road, Hastings for the shooting of the film "Grey Owl" starring Pierce Brosnan **[40]**.

The film was based on the true story of Archie Belaney, a larger-than-life character who became known as Grey Owl; born in Hastings in 1888 he moved to Canada in 1906 where as a Beaver trapper on the big lakes he joined the Indian way of life, his childhood dream. Later, he became known as one of the world's first champions of wildlife conservation before passing away suddenly in 1938.

EMPRESS COACHES
British & Continental Coach Travel
Private Coach Hire
Coaches available 27 to 53 Seaters
Disabled Facilities available on Mini Coaches
10 / 11 St Margarets Road,
St Leonards, East Sussex TN 37 6EH
Telephone: (01424) 430621
WE ARE ***HERE***......TO GET YOU ***THERE***.

Business card. 1998

Actor Pierce Brosnan played the part convincingly, and when we were not engaged on running the director, staff and newly-run reels of film from location to the Cinque Ports Hotel in Hastings for screening and editing, watching the progress of the shoot was very interesting. One of our drivers at the time, Ray Howard, and I shared the driving, and with the last day of location filming nearly over, one of the crew enquired if it were possible for Ray to source fish and chips (take-away of course) for the entire crew on the location. Ray, to all who knew him, was a versatile man of means and immediately despatched himself to find somewhere to provide a very large order at a busy period of the day. After some surprise from the willing proprietor of a local business on the size and speed required of the order, Ray duly came back fully loaded with varied supplies! I recall how, amidst all the crew being under a fair amount of pressure to get the filming 'in the can', Pierce Brosnan was always remarkably composed, and Lord Attenborough very pleasant and unassuming.

The fleet had grown to 11 vehicles, with no less than seven different manufacturers represented within it, including Bedford, Omni, Freight Rover, Ford, DAF, Renault and Toyota - not an ideal operating situation, but necessary because of the quite varied type of work commitments we had.

With what had become a large fleet of various sized vehicles, Jan was keen for us to diversify the business, so a fresh attempt was made to launch back again into the day excursions market. Brochures with a good varied mix of full and half-day excursions were offered, and although popular the loadings were smaller than anticipated, and combined with the increase in private hire, with all the additional work involved it was decided not to continue these after the 1998 season.

Jan certainly had many industry changes to accommodate, not least changes in the law concerning the fitting of seat belts on coaches. Although new regulations had come into place in 1995, there were amended requirements concerning the way in which seats should be fixed to floors and extra strength on seat legs needed in case of accidents.

Additional modifications to comply with all of this were needed to virtually all of the fleet, and the services of engineers Bill and Mark Sweetman were engaged to perform this large engineering task, not made any easier because of the broad range of vehicles owned.

41

42

43

44

45

46

Chapter 6:

Stephen Dine takes over – Dream becomes reality.

By the start of the 1999 season Jan's other business interests were becoming more varied and time-consuming, and it was at this time I approached Jan with a view to purchasing Empress Coaches Ltd. A deal was reached between us, with the idea of my taking over in the September, although we worked together until the company was finally signed over on the night of 20 December 1999. It was only two days later that my wife Jayne gave birth to our first child, a son Joshua, on 22 December.

To emphasis that Empress was once more a real family business, the sign-writing on the rear of most of the current fleet was modified from 2000 so that above Empress Coaches Ltd. we added "Stephen Dine & Son" (see **[102]** in the photographs section) – until the arrival of Bethany four years later when to avoid complications we reverted to just the company name. Fleet numbers so treated were 38, 40 and 41 (following repaints), and nos. 50 to 63 with the exception of 51 and 61.

One of my work colleagues, Peter Pragnell agreed to take on responsibility for assisting in the running of the office and administration in our early years, something we did with the fresh enthusiasm of a new chapter in the Empress story. Peter later went on to become leader of Hastings Borough Council. Harry Phillips and Sid Lovell, also working colleagues and friends, both now retired from coach driving, although still helping out at the depot, were also pleased to see the company moving ahead.

To help with the initial purchase of my new business, three vehicles not engaged on contract work were sold to help finances in the early stages. Fleet numbers 38, 48, and 49 left for new owners in Wales, Wigan and Cambridgeshire respectively, bringing the fleet down to a more manageable seven vehicles at that time. To begin the fleet restructure a Dormobile-bodied Ford transit (L760 SDY) was purchased from Bexhill Community Bus, becoming fleet no. 50, and with the help of Bill Sweetman it was refurbished as a 20-seat coach, filling the gap left by the sale of the Toyota 21-seater. Dormobile had actually certified that particular type of vehicle and body combination as a 20-seater if required; it proved to be a very useful size for us.

At this time fleet number 38, the 41-seat Bedford (A843 XFW) was the only large coach left, and it soon became apparent that for the 2000 season this would not be enough to cover the company's commitments. Viewing various vehicles in the 45 to 53 seat range, I travelled to numerous operators across the country and was dismayed by the general condition of vehicles being offered for sale.

41 Three of the fleet at Worth Abbey in June 2001: J397 KOR, DBB 127V, and A843 XFW.

42 Stephen Dine carrying out maintenance on JAZ 1066 in the depot.

43 The "Battle of Hastings" livery on D36 ALR (BHZ 1066) in 2001.

44 The Queen's Golden Jubilee livery on J430 WFA with Stephen Dine and "Prince William" in April 2002.

45 The four Omnis at The Oval Hastings bus rally in May 2003.

46 The two Optare Aleros purchased from Rye Community Transport, in Sea Road, St. Leonards in December 2006.

On returning home, thinking about finding a good clean vehicle, I decided to contact Scotland & Bates in Appledore, Kent to see if they had anything for sale. They did indeed have a Bedford Plaxton (EBM 460T), which had been new to them 21 years earlier. For its age it was in very good condition, and helped to bridge the gap that had been left by the sale of the DAF. At the time the then new "T" registration plates had just been released; ironically this coach, although T registered, was from the first time around in 1979! I did have some fun with our regular customers when discussing bookings on the telephone by letting them know always that I would make sure we put on our new 'T' registered vehicle just for them!

I had always been on the lookout for new ideas to promote the company, and struck on a good one when the opportunity arose to purchase a cherished registration number for our fleet number 52 back in 2000. The practice of using dateless registration plates is far from novel, especially in the coach industry, I had found the number plate JAZ 1066 for sale with a dealer, and found it too good to resist. For obvious reasons, with Empress being a Hastings-based operator, what better reason to purchase?

Over the next few years, with some searching just for fun as time allowed, when a 1066 number plate became available another one would be purchased for a member of the fleet. The prefixes were normally of Irish origin and eventually some gems came our way - now our fleet was advertising Empress Coaches from the 1066 Country. The only English registration issue available at the time, a 1932 Leeds number (UG 1066) was more interesting as originally on a motorcycle; it was being sold separately from the bike due to its owner's emigrating permanently to South Africa, therefore the registration on it would have been of no further use. The purchase price covered the shipping costs of the bike to its new life overseas.

Occasionally a particular vehicle proves to become an interesting purchase. In June 2000 I visited a dealer in Peterborough with Colin from Rambler Coaches to look casually at stock out of interest. He had gone to purchase back a 29-seat Bedford that was originally new to them in 1983, and I noticed a forlorn 35-seat Bedford YLQ Plaxton (DBB 127V) which was parked in the corner of the yard. Although badly hand-painted, it looked as if it would be an interesting project to refurbish it for a school run and some local private hire because of its handy 8-metre length. I made a silly offer on it, which with small negotiation was accepted a week later and the vehicle was collected.

Delving into the vehicle's history it was found to have had eight previous owners, and it turned out that 20 years before, it had been delivered new to the London company Armchair, luxuriously appointed with reclining seats, air-conditioning, toilet, servery and full draw curtains. Later it had been purchased by another London company, Spirit of London, and in their ownership it had appeared in an episode of the TV series Inspector Morse entitled "Deceived by Flight" starring John Thaw and Kevin Whately. The coach appeared in various scenes travelling from Oxford to Dover Docks.

Later in the year I had been tipped off by Dews Coaches in Cambridgeshire, with whom we were quite friendly, that a really nice clean 53 seater Bedford YNT (D77 HRU) was probably available from the operator Fowlers at Holbeach Drove. I went to have a look and just had

to buy, as it was a huge leap in profile for our fleet. It even had a custom-built stainless steel exhaust system fitted!

Dews were interested in our old Bedford EBM 460T, and after doing a deal we all agreed to meet at Dew's depot in Somersham to do the exchanges. 2000 was a particularly wet year and September/October was no exception. I set off with Jayne and Joshua, who was only 10 months old at the time, from Hastings in EBM but only got as far as Bewl Water on the A 21 when the delays started. The village of Lamberhurst was under water through flooding, and I eventually managed to turn around, travelling across country via Goudhurst, which was also partially flooded, until the weather on the journey eventually improved until we arrived in the Cambridgeshire sunshine. Our greeting party hardly believed how bad the weather was down south! The journey back proved to be no better; in fact I diverted via the M20 and Maidstone, travelling in the torrential rain that had caused many other villages including most of the land around Bodiam to be under water.

Customers at this time included, Shearbarn Holiday Park, Hastings; Don Minter from Boston College, London; the Masonic Widows; SARAH (Stroke Association); Michael Tyler Furniture & Strome House. **[41]**

The following year, 2001, I was becoming a bit more experimental with ideas on the new versions of our livery. The Bedford that we had purchased from Fowlers looked so good with its vinyl graphics of bouncing balls on its sides that I had left this in place and just added our fleet names **[42]**. The idea of something with the "1066 Country" theme seemed good, and eventually the idea of Harold came about. We had purchased another Bedford, this time a 41-seater in Wales (D36 ALR), so decided to experiment. I liked the end result of Harold with the famous arrow in his eye, accompanied by a Norman knight on horseback, depicted on both sides of the coach, and of course my new design was worthy of picture and text in the local Hastings Observer Newspaper **[43]**.

Things didn't stop there, and the following year in 2002 Britain celebrated the Queen's Golden Jubilee. This was too good an opportunity to miss, so when purchasing a refurbished Mercedes (J430 WFA) from the dealer Houston Ramm in Rochdale, I enquired whether they could paint it metallic gold. Answer from them - no problem! I recall sitting up in central London one late night on a two-coach private hire booking with one of our drivers Dave Tune, reading his newspaper in amusement whilst parked, I thought up ideas on a simple but effective design to honour Her Majesty. Duly faxed over to the dealer the following day, the design was interpreted onto the bus by a graphics company, so I didn't actually see the results until it was delivered to our depot on the back of a low-loader from Lancashire. I hadn't mentioned the one-off livery to any of the other staff so I don't know who was more surprised when the vehicle arrived, them or me!

The vehicle's arrival into the fleet was marked not only by the then Mayor of Hastings, Cllr. Jackie Dowling, but also "Prince William" (hired in look-alike of course) to view the new acquisition and give it the "Royal" approval, and again this vehicle featured in the local newspaper **[44]**. That year the coach saw extensive use to many popular destinations, and also visited Althorp House, resting place of Princess Diana, on a private hire.

At this time we had a fairly good pattern of work, the school runs, private hire and a small amount of tendered bus work making up the mainstay of our business.

Back in the June of 2002 a surprise purchase was of a 1972 Bedford VAL twin-steer 53-seater (NEC 237K), a type of vehicle made famous by films such as "The Italian Job" and "Magical Mystery Tour". I had passed my PSV driving test in one of these vehicles long ago in August 1989, so when three late examples had been withdrawn by Abbeyways Coaches in Halifax, I purchased one via well-known operator/enthusiast Paul Emery. Delivered by Paul Saunter's Haulage on his low-loader, we stored the vehicle at the Cross Inn at Staplecross, Kent, then the home of Monk's Coaches and with Jason Monk, set to work in our spare time making it roadworthy for full Class 6 MOT. I did actually use the VAL on school runs that season as well as attending some commercial vehicle rallies including the Bedford Gathering at Cambridge, where they were also celebrating 40 years since the introduction of the VAL in 1962.

In the early part of 2002 we had been approached by the committee, consisting mainly of local publicans, who organised the annual Icklesham Village Beer Festival (IVBF) over the last weekend of July, with a view to our providing a shuttle bus service to and from Hastings and Rye to the venue situated in the large field next to the "Robin Hood". It would be a completely unknown quantity for us, whether the takings would be good, although feedback on revellers wanting to get home, especially late in the evenings the previous year, suggested it should be. It could not be run as a private hire booking as the IVBF needed to get some of the cost back by charging so the only logical (and legal) way was my suggestion to register the three-day event as a scheduled service with a flat fare, which we did. We still had an adequate supply of Almex ticket machines available to use. One small vehicle operated from Rye & Rye Harbour, with two vehicles from Hastings. Our hopes that it would be popular were correct, and we had steady loadings especially on the Saturday night return journeys where another one of our fleet was drafted in from the end of its previous booking as a duplicate to help clear the overflow passengers. It must have ranked as one of the most elusive bus services ever operated in the local area as it started and ceased operation within three days.

The service ran again the following year with the benefit of some previous statistics on how to make slight improvements to the sizes of vehicle used at different parts of the day, and the timetables; I borrowed another bus with seating for 53 and standing capacity for 20 to help move the enormous numbers leaving on the late Saturday night finish. I remember having to restrain the last people from getting on the almost certainly overloaded old Bedford bus as it started raining late on the busiest night. After leaving Icklesham, knowing the steep White Hart Hill just outside Hastings had to be tackled a couple of miles up the road, I tried to get a run at it, although the long drag of the hill cut the speed of the bus almost straight away. It's one of the rare occasions where you know, as the engine revs are about to die off on the steepest part of the hill, not to miss the last gear changing down (of 1st crawler) as otherwise it would mean disembarking nearly eighty merry people off in the dark to walk up the hill so you could get moving again!

Customers this year included, Silverhill Club, Unilock, ITS language school, The University of the Third Age, & Daisy Roots Morris Dancers.

Our Bedford VAL was normally parked at the former Broomham School in Guestling, re-named by its new owner Giles Sutton 'Buckswood', and with two other coaches there, space was now at a premium, with Giles having quite rightly new ideas for additional classrooms and facilities to improve the school, so his kind offer of additional parking was becoming understandably limited. Our depot site was also very constricted, so the decision to sell the VAL in February 2003 was one which had regretfully to be made.

It was part-exchanged in a deal with dealer Houston Ramm, including the 'Harold' Bedford, against a neat Autobus Classique-bodied Mercedes 814 33-seater (M351 TDO). Also thrown in on the deal was a scruffy OBC Omni welfare bus that they had not been able to sell (K297 UKR). As we already had three of the type, I thought it would be useful as a source of spares, although when the vehicle arrived it proved to be in such good overall condition we prepared it for an MOT and ran it for a year. Sprayed in our traditional livery, I had our new website address displayed in large letters on its sides with "easy access coach" below it; this was before the local bus company coincidentally applied a similar logo for their low-floor vehicles. We were now running four of these Omnis **[45]**.

2003 also saw the launch of our first web-site www.empressofhastings.co.uk. One of our drivers Jez Lamb had been working on various ideas before designing and building the final product. The results were fantastic, and I admit that at the time I had not initially realised what a powerful advertising and marketing tool a web-site would be. The simpler web-address, empresscoaches.com was already in use with our namesake company in London so we decided, as the lettering applied on the sides of our vehicles – "Empress of Hastings" was a fairly direct statement of who we were, why not use the same branding with the web-site. The www.empresscoaches.com domain name did eventually become available, so the original one was gradually phased out. It may be worth mentioning that there is no connection between ourselves and Empress Motors Ltd. of east London, although the history of this quality operator dates back even further than ours to 1923.

A new school contract from Westfield through the lanes to Claverham Community College at Battle was secured in September 2003. The last time that I had driven on a schools run to Claverham was back in the 1990 season when I had worked for a short time for Cooks Coaches of Westfield. Cooks had served Claverham since it opened as Battle County Secondary School at Easter 1955. For many years the contracts had remained with them, and back in 1990 nearly all of the vehicles working the school contracts were Cooks, apart from the odd additional operator and an elderly Autopoint double-decker bus from Herstmonceux. By 2003 the double-decker had been replaced by a minibus, and the other vehicles waiting to collect pupils in the school grounds were from Rambler and J&H Coaches of Rye. How times change.

In the September of that year the decision was made to sell the 53-seat Bedford. With much airport and transfer work, and the occasional tours that we operated, luggage space and was at a premium. Even though the Bedford had had large custom-built side lockers built by Bill Sweetman,

we were struggling for space to fit all of the passengers' luggage on board. The popularity of moulded plastic suitcases had not helped, as unlike the traditional type of suitcase they do not have any flexibility, so cannot be squeezed in tightly into the boot space and therefore filled the inadequate room even quicker.

One of our regular drivers at the time, John Foster, returned from a tour with a local bowls group, only just managing to fit everything on board. Thinking back to the rear-engined DAF from Jan Auer's days, with its excellent luggage capacity, gave me thoughts about a vehicle which had always been a favourite of mine, a Mercedes-Benz 0303 integral with a 14.6 litre V8 engine. I had always liked the shape and design of them, and with its German build quality I thought "let's have one for a while". After the Bedford, it was a completely different vehicle (HBZ 4673). Sourced from a company in West Yorkshire, although it looked fine, it had had a hard life as we later found out, but after bringing the vehicle up to our standard and adorning it with a fade-in Maroon to Ivory paintwork it did look good.

The Bedford had left for a new life in Hereford with Heardmans Coaches, and I was personally sorry to see it go as it had been a really good vehicle, and with it ended more than sixty years of continuous Bedford ownership in the fleet.

The Mercedes eventually settled in well and although I initially spent quite a bit on improvements it was a lovely vehicle drive and never let us down. It became the next JAZ1066.

On 6 March 2004 my wife Jayne gave birth to our second child Bethany, I remember a well-wisher saying to us "congratulations, a pigeon pair now". We had not heard that expression before.

As the company was celebrating 75 years of trading that year, we managed to get the whole fleet together, including my preserved Triumph Courier Van (in its Company colours) to show off to the public for the Hastings Bus Rally on the Oval. We had a pleasant surprise in the form of a visit from Harry Phillips junior, who came up to view the fleet with his wife May. At that same moment, coincidentally, local enthusiast Bob Cook also came over to us and produced a marvellous photograph that he had obtained of the coach in which Harry had passed his PSV driving test back in 1946, until then a vehicle of which we had no photographic records. May Phillips sadly passed away just two months later.

We finally ceased regular stage service operation on 20 August 2004 when the 347 Pett - Hastings route was due for a new tender; it was taken on by Coastal Coaches. I was not personally unhappy, as I had always felt that we were never really suited to stage carriage because of the types of vehicles we operated and because we were a relatively small operator not large enough to accommodate the dedicated type of 'bus' within our fleet. I feel that bus routes should be left to larger companies which specialise in that type of operation.

We were finding that the smaller members of the fleet were certainly the busiest as far as all year round work goes. With the cost of fuel gradually rising, the Mercedes 0303 was proving an increasingly thirsty vehicle to run, so in October 2004 my mind was finally set on selling it as I felt that the market for a vehicle of that size within our fleet was still shrinking. After its sale the largest vehicle in line up for the 2005 season was the 33-seater (M351 TDO, now re-

Empress Coaches
– ESTABLISHED 1929 –
Proprietor: Stephen Dine
Private Hire – Contract Hire a Speciality
10 - 11 St Margaret's Road, St Leonards-on-Sea
East Sussex TN37 6EH
Tel/Fax: 01424 430621
www.empressofhastings.co.uk

Business card. 2004

registered BHZ 1066) That year we got by without the larger coach, and it was interesting to see how our running costs diminished quite dramatically with the 0303's departure. My philosophy has always been that if a vehicle cannot justify a good return and a stand-up in the fleet on its own then it goes. I have never believed in flagship vehicles that have to be paid for by the hard working other members of the fleet unless they actually operate on profitable charters.

That year we also picked up an interesting booking with the 33-seater to Germany. The customer had seen our vehicle at Dover docks, liked it, telephoned us for a price and booked it. I think that it was the first time Empress had been to Germany, though we later transported students, and a film crew to Bremen for eight days.

Into the 2005 season, with the usual sets of goals to achieve for the year, including promising myself not to buy any more vehicles for the time being and just to concentrate on running the existing ones, I got as far as 4th January before bidding and successfully purchasing an Alexander-bodied Mercedes Benz 709 25-seat bus from Alan Lewis at Stagecoach South. Knowing that this was size suited our fleet, I thought instead of buying an overpriced re-seated example from a dealer we would re-furbish one in-house to our standard. With drivers John Foster and Philip Semple having time between school runs due to the quiet time of year, they stripped out the whole interior ready for it to receive new headlining, floor and a brand new set of coach seats for the coming season.

Bill Sweetman had crafted a new Mercedes Vario front panel onto it, to give it a "new look" and it had been re-sprayed in our livery. As the vehicle had been retrofitted with coach seats and seat belts, it had to be re-certified at the time. Bill and I had already checked with the certifying officer at the test station on the correct bolts and fixings to go through the floor to hold the legs down tight underneath to the body members, with the only stipulation being that we make sure to use penny washers on the bolts before tightening up the seats to the underneath. On presentation of the vehicle for test, to my surprise the vehicle failed, only on the size of washers used under the floor, and on questioning his decision by showing the certifying officer a penny piece and similar sized washer from my pocket he said "I meant an old penny!." I was born the year our coinage went decimal, as was pointed out to the certifying officer; even so all the bolts had to be undone again to fit the larger washers.

At this time a custom-built luggage trailer was purchased that could hold twenty five cases and could be towed by the 16-seater or either of the 25-seat vehicles for transfer work. It proved to be very useful.

The same year we re-tendered for and again won the four Glyne Gap School contracts with the county council. I was relieved, as they were a large piece of our work, and I have never been complacent about people against whom you might be tendering. With this thoughts of the two remaining Omnis came to light, as we were still running the original pair bought by Tony Patten back in 1990, and at some stage they would need replacing. Both had enjoyed long periods of time within the fleet, being absolutely ideal for the type of work they were designed for. The security of the new contracts made me look again to update them.

Tony Patten and I drove to Wigan and back via Essex, looking at potential vehicles and we finally found and bought a clean Iveco with an automatic gearbox (P639 ROU), and a few days afterwards I travelled down to Bridport in Dorset where a Mercedes Vario was sourced (R128 AWF). In some ways it felt like a backward step, as the vehicles purchased were not low-floor and were equipped with external tail lifts. The plan was that the two Omnis now would only run on until the end of the July term.

After leaving Bridport I travelled back up the coast, stopping at Weymouth to look at a second-hand Volvo B9M 41-seater for sale. The larger coach issue had been on my mind since the 0303 had been sold. Although the 33-seater was doing fine, we were losing out on some bookings, although usually only by a few seats; also the luggage capacity on our 33-seater could nowhere near cater for a full load, although I didn't want another full-size coach. The 10 metre Bedfords we had run over the years were always an ideal size, so I continued a relaxed search, preferably for a Volvo to purchase.

Sometimes when you are looking at vehicles it takes you to unusual locations to find them. I travelled up to London to view another B9M, and after querying the final directions I arrived at a Jewish Cemetery where the coach was indeed, as stated, parked inside the cemetery gates. It was apparently the operating base for the vehicle.

Eventually a very clean Dennis Javelin with 41-seat Wadham Stringer coachwork was purchased from Witham SV, a dealer in Grantham, Lincs. which specialised in ex-Ministry of Defence disposals. There was a selection to choose from, and after I had made a poor salesman jumpstart every vehicle so that I could hear the Cummins engines running I picked the one which had been used from new by RAF Brize Norton.

Amongst various other items in the huge yard, including tanks, motorcycles and staff cars, there was a large gathering of the famous Bedford 'green goddess' fire engines that were now all redundant, with a trade price of around £3000, but I resisted the temptation to bring one back as well as the coach.

Of course the significance of purchasing the Dennis was that it was only the second time Empress had operated this particular make of vehicle, the first one being the original coach in 1929. The new Dennis had never been registered for civilian use, and after a few headaches between driving to DVLA in Brighton, and the Department for Transport Testing Station in Hastings, it eventually received its first new registration mark, our GAZ 1066.

Customers that year included, St Michaels Hospice, Virgin Vee, Kay Cornford's Welcome Club, Blue Arrow Recruitment, Vacuum Generators and Watermens Close residents.

Towards the end 2006 an opportunity arose to purchase two Optare Alero minibuses that had been operated from new by Rye Community Transport. I had only really wanted one, for its low-floor concept, although a good deal was struck on purchasing the pair (consecutively registered YR02 YTG and YTH) **[46]** so we bought these stylish-looking 16 seaters. Features included air-conditioning, dark tinted windows, and a completely flat floor fully tracked to accommodate wheelchair users.

Empress Coaches

ESTABLISHED 1929

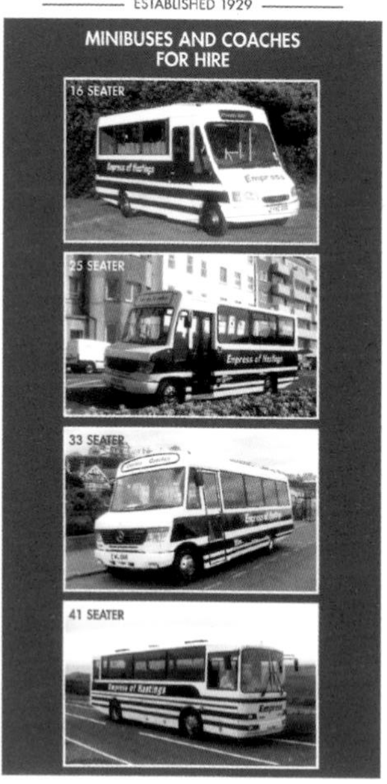

Tel / Fax: 01424 430621
E-Mail: info@empresscoaches.com
www.empresscoaches.com

Mail shot flyer 2006 season

Very modern looking vehicles, on their arrival at the depot they certainly made the rest of the fleet look old overnight. After being painted in our livery they both received our personalised registration numbers 1066, becoming WIL and JIL; that seemed appropriate. Business at this time had been flourishing and the timing of the Aleros joining the fleet certainly enhanced it. 2006 had been a year of many industry changes, with others to come, and the forthcoming 2008 LEZ (low emission zone) regulations for commercial vehicles travelling in and out of central London were something that had to be addressed if as an operator we were to continue to travel to the capital. At the time it was uncertain what types of vehicles would be initially affected by new emissions regulations, and I felt the time was right to sell our 25-seater Mercedes in favour of a newer Toyota 26-seater vehicle which could be made to comply.

Regulars this year included, the local Mayor's office, Percy Walker (Solicitors), Sheppard Place in Battle and Pinelands Language School.

On 20 March 2007 Harry Phillips junior passed away in his eighty-second year. He had been lost without his late wife May. A true gentleman, with his dry 'Sussex' humour, he was sadly missed. Harry was unique that not only had he previously owned Empress Coaches but had also worked for all four of the Company's other owners over his 57 years driving **[47]**. Harry's funeral service in St Mary Star-of-the-Sea Church, where he and May had been married and were regular worshippers for many years, was a time of reflection, and I was humbled as, when his coffin processed from the church at the end of the service with his family following close behind, Harry's son Peter stopped and handed me Harry's PSV driver's badge, something he had worn throughout his long career with Empress.

Looking back over that year, it was probably the most difficult one I had yet experienced. Anyone involved in business, and especially the transport industry, will know that sometimes it doesn't seem to matter how hard you are working to keep it all running as smoothly as possible, nevertheless the problems do not let up. These trying times seem to come and go in cycles. For some time it had been in the back of my head to streamline the types and sizes of vehicles we were running, and with the difficulties of having the Dennis off the road three times in the middle of the summer season due to continually waiting for spares, I was becoming more and more convinced that I should finally specialise in what had become our recognised niche market of the smaller types of vehicle.

We had always had around nine to ten vehicles in the fleet at any one time; our depot being compact, could only house six, including the Dennis. Fortunately three of our regular drivers always kept their minibuses at home during term time, although in the holiday periods they all came back to the depot. We had been fortunate in having a kind offer for some years from Pat Angel & John Steadman at Moorhurst Residential Home in Westfield to keep our out-of-use minibuses there in the holidays, but that year Moorhurst was closing, so a new place had to be found.

With early signs that all might not be well with the national economy in the future which could mean less private hire off-season, I made the difficult decision to sell off the last of the large coaches from the fleet for the time being. My feeling was right, as after the Dennis had left towards the end of the summer season in the September for a new operator in Scotland,

enquiries for it were only occasional. I felt that if the market for full size coaches opens up again in the future for us, then we would certainly take the opportunity.
At the same time my thoughts also turned to the Aleros, which although fantastic-looking vehicles, were plagued with the same main problems as the Dennis - poor parts back-up supply, and difficult suppliers. One thing that we had not envisaged as such a problem was that the incredibly long wheelbases on an Alero made it more than a difficult machine to use in and around the side streets of Hastings. If cars were parked on corners of streets, sometimes we literally got stuck as we couldn't make the turn! With one of them off the road for eight weeks due to a suspected computer-based problem, the writing was on the wall for a long-term stay in the fleet.
We still had one of the original Omnis that was now really meant to be a spare/back up vehicle although it was still out on the road more than one of the Aleros. Later in 2007 two late Ford Transits with coach built bodies (T174 BVV and V403 BNH) were sourced, and after refurbishment they took the place of the Aleros and the operating headaches that went with them. I heard that, the following year, one of the Aleros had started off with its new owner quite well for the first few months until a suspension part was needed, then spent the next three months off the road due to a back order of this part not arriving at Optare. I felt genuine frustration and sympathy for the operator over this ridiculous predicament.
Towards the end of the year the Omni was treated to its first full re-spray to smarten it up again, really as a mark of respect for what had certainly become a fully paid up member of the fleet.
Regular customers with us included Janet Sinden Solicitors, Mrs. Catt & Ladies, Sidley Day Centre and Conquest Sports & Social Club.
Work began in early 2008 on a new workshop at the rear of the depot by the very able Mark Saunters, with the old one being converted into an office for me. The other half of the rear depot wall was taken out, and the roof extended, to make two more parking spaces for vehicles, so that when the school runs were off there was enough room for all of the fleet at the depot.
Of course it wasn't long before I had spotted something for sale; it was not too big and would fit nicely in the corner of the depot along with our long serving Omni. I travelled up to York to meet a gentleman by the name of Dick Craven, local garage proprietor and former 1960s motorcycle grass-track racing champion. On meeting, he casually mentioned that he still held the speed record in drag racing for the fastest person on a British bike still fitted with road tyres, on a 1000cc Vincent at 122 mph.
My twin brother Paul (a motorcycle enthusiast himself), and I were treated to a private tour of Dick's extensive collection of bikes, many of which, including his legendary police bikes, were in regular use with Yorkshire Television on location for the TV series Heartbeat and The Royal. I was pleased to purchase what I had gone for - a 1967 Bedford CA Utilabus with a Martin Walter 11 seat body (XPT 454F). It had also appeared on these programmes, and just happened to be painted in a pleasant cream and maroon livery not unlike ours.

Originally with a petrol engine, at some stage in the 1970s this had been replaced with a Perkins diesel unit, which, with the alterations in gearing, gave it a maximum speed of 38 mph, so the long drive back to Hastings took a steady nine and a half hours. Once again a Bedford was back in the fleet.

In February I decided to look for something around the 29 seats size, preferably with larger boot space than the Toyota could offer, and after much searching across the country at various coach dealers and operators a nice Mercedes 814 with an Autobus Nouvelle 29-seat body (V7 PCC) was purchased from an operator in Forfar, Scotland after I flew up to view it.

On the 31 March my father (who is still driving for us) and I took out the Arthritis Care Club, one of our long-standing regular customers, for the very last time, as the club was disbanding locally. Although an enjoyable lunch was had by all at the Langham Hotel in Eastbourne, it was with some sadness that I felt that we would not be picking them up any more.

Dad used the Mercedes 29-seater, and I drove the Omni, a vehicle with which they were certainly familiar as it had been one of their regular vehicles for eighteen years and, with its low floor step arrangement, was always appreciated. Betty Marshall had played many important roles within the committee over her 33 years involvement, and I always enjoyed our Monday morning chat on the telephone every second week throughout the years to discuss that day's transport requirements and pick-ups for the two vehicles to the centre where they met as a group. We had been providing their transport for so long that Betty could not actually remember when our association started, although our records did show bookings back at least to 1979 every Tuesday when under their original name of the Bristol Rheumatic and Arthritic Association before latterly becoming 'Arthritis Care'.

A new school run started on 21 April 2008, picking up just one student with special needs from Mayfield to take him to a school in Tonbridge, Kent on a daily basis. Normally this is a job too small for us, although we were the only operator to provide a quotation for the journey so an 8-seat Mercedes Benz Vito (V74 GKH) was purchased specially for the job. In July we were again asked to provide transport for one student on a home-to-school basis; he required a bespoke vehicle that could accommodate a large wheelchair. A fully accessible Citroen Dispatch (WV51 ZZG) was sourced to meet the need, complete with professionally converted inside sloping floor and fold-out rear access ramp, perfect for the pupil's needs. Again, a slight departure from our regular requests.

The rising operating costs were certainly biting in 2008, not least the price of diesel fuel. Although we had an extremely slow start to the year, the summer period had been surprisingly busy, and with this in mind I had made contact with a coach dealer in the middle of the year to look into the possibility of having a new 35-seater in the fleet for the 2009 season, to coincide with the 80th anniversary of the company. Prospects of purchasing one looked good at first, although with the worsening state of the global economy later in the summer, the idea now seemed rather bold, not knowing what 2009 would bring. It seemed ironic that nearly eighty years earlier, Harry Phillips had purchased his first coach, and a new one at that, not long before the famous Wall Street crash, and here I was contemplating my first new coach, but this time knowing in advance that it might not be a wise move.

After much careful consideration the plans were put on hold, although still wanting to provide something newer to the fleet profile, I decided later in the year to update with another 16-seater, probably one of our most popular types. I found a potential vehicle, and at short notice booked a flight in March, again by coincidence to Edinburgh as I had previously done, to collect a late type air-conditioned Mercedes-Benz Soroco (R16 CTC) from a company based there.

Also at this time we were fortunate to finally have the services of engineer Bill Sweetman with us on a permanent basis to look after our maintenance. Vehicle maintenance to a high standard is vital to delivering the overall package, and Bill's years of experience are invaluable.

In late 2008 a new interim livery had been experimented with on fleet numbers 80 & 77 in an effort to raise the image of the private hire fleet. Although it was pleasant, with a mainly white scheme, and minimal logos, I felt that we were not really creating much of an impact with our new vehicles. In the December I spoke about it to fellow businessman Luca Venditto from the Italian Way Restaurant in Hastings, who had chartered one of the vehicles, and he introduced me to local marketing consultant Graham How for ideas on how to move forward.

Meeting in early 2009, Graham quickly saw the need for us to make changes and to re-brand the fleet, with a new corporate livery for the private hire vehicles. With the talents of Graham and designer Cliff Brooker, a new look was created in April 2009 with fleet number 81, recently purchased from an operator in Somerset, being immediately repainted into the new prestige fleet colours of claret and cream. The idea was to keep the strong local awareness of our traditional livery, but to modernise and create more impact for a 21st century look.

Not long after, fleet numbers 80 and the newly acquired 82 were both treated to the new livery, giving us that much needed visual appeal with these smart vehicles. With the recession biting hard, I felt Graham's clever marketing and the new fleet profile gave us a much better summer season than I had anticipated.

The Bedford CA had been unfortunately sold towards the end of April, due to the promise of a new contract that never materialised, although it proved a good omen as the two vehicles originally purchased for this were soon in demand as the season took off.

The first of the contract members of the fleet, No 68, was refurbished and painted towards the end of August 2009 with another of Cliff's re-designs to re-brand our non private-hire vehicles as Empress Contract Hire.

It seemed to make sense, as in recent years we have run a varied fleet and it had been confusing on occasions to regular and potential customers as to what type and specification of coach they might be hiring. As time allows, the plan is to apply the new liveries when updating or repainting the other vehicles.

So what of the years ahead? Who knows what 21st. century opportunities will become available to Empress. Markets and the industry, as you have read, do change and part of our success has been the ability to adapt with it.

Here's looking forward to the next opportunity.

We hope you have been enlightened to our first eighty years.

47 Stephen Dine in 2005 with Tony Patten (right) and Harry Edwin Phillips (1925 - 2007), one-time owner who had also worked for all the four other owners of "Empress" in the course of 57 years driving.

48 CAZ 1066, on a wet day in Hastings, October 2009 wearing new contract hire livery.

Appendix I – Personal Memories
Phyllis Phillips

Phyllis Phillips, daughter of 'old' Harry and Ethel, is now Mrs. Lapworth and lives in retirement in Hampshire. She has been kind enough to read through the draft of the early history and has related in Chapter 2 her recollections of visiting her Aunt Helen at Hellingly Hospital using the 'Cuckoo Line" in the days before the first coach was purchased.

Phyllis's memory of childhood rides in the coach are evocative of the pleasures of coach trips in the 1930s: "I remember going on lots of coach trips, and once on the way back from Rye the coach could not get up White Hart Hill, and all the passengers except me had to get out and push. Once on a trip to the Rother Valley I rolled into a ditch full of stinging nettles and wailed uncontrollably. In an effort to quieten me I was taken into the Rother Valley Hotel where my stings were treated with dock leaves, and I was allowed to play with some Dalmatian puppies".

"On a trip to Brighton Races I remember meeting the famous tipster 'Prince Monolulu' – a black man with feathers in his hair, and he gave me an orange".

"During World War 2 on the way back from Hellingly Hospital we stopped to watch a German air attack on the Radar Station on Pevensey Marshes. The coach was also used to carry hop-pickers from rural villages to Samuel West's hop gardens in the Peasmarsh or Iden area, and during the Battle of Britain a German plane was shot down not far away, the British pilot doing a Victory roll overhead and we all cheered".

Her brother, 'young' Harry, recalled how Phyllis had fallen into the excavation for the fuel tank at the new garage. Mrs Lapworth's husband Rufus later drove for Tony Patten during the 1970s and 1980s.

Harold Corke

In 2006 at the age of 94, Harold Corke gave his own memories of the early days of the Phillips' first coach, when, as a teenager who had just started work, he played and scored for Hastings Ramblers Cricket Club, the first group of passengers to travel in the new Dennis. His father had instigated the club. Among the other passengers were Police Inspector A. Small; Frank Dann – a railway official; Frank Watson, a solicitor's clerk; George Corke, a greengrocer on the West Hill; Billy Hawes of the Hastings Observer; Bill Michener and a Mr. Ray. With 11 in the team and all the extras the coach was already overloaded! The early destinations included Icklesham, Pett, Winchelsea; all short trips so the income from hiring probably did not even cover running costs, but the owner Harry Phillips was one of the team and that was all that mattered to him.

Stephen Dine

As a young lad, with my twin brother Paul I would walk home from All Saints School, just across the road from the Empress garage but I have no recollections of taking a special interest or really realising what was there.

It was later, in December 1982 at the family home in Harold Road when one weekend looking out of the front room window I started to notice these two coaches running at regular separate intervals past the house (we lived on a main bus route). It later appeared that Empress had been hired over the Christmas holiday that year by Debenhams for their shoppers' free bus service. I liked the livery of maroon and white, and the older vehicle of the pair had an added visual appeal due to its distinctive 1960s shape.

Not really understanding who Empress were, after we both started at Hillcrest Secondary school in 1983, I began to see more of these Empress vehicles out on the road in what seemed all different sizes, some in a newer orange, red & white livery. I suppose it was then that I began to take an interest as a 'coach-spotter' (a very un-trendy word in the 21st century!) or enthusiast as, instinctively you start to take notes on registrations, colours etc. just for fun, just for something to do.

Most days walking to school, we would see the Bedford DHN 455C waiting to collect the old ladies from Barrington House in Ore Village to go to their day centre. We gradually built up good humour (and cheek) with the drivers and eventually got into some evening and weekend cleaning work mainly at the St Margaret's Road depot, also at Githa Road.

Drivers who in the early days helped to mould my ideas as an impressionable teenager included Harry Phillips, Jim Glasgow, Sid Lovell, Bill Relph, John Collier, George Stephenson, Bill Batchelor, and John Heath to name a few.

On leaving school, I went for an interview as an apprentice sign-writer, as I did have talents with art at school. However with thoughts of it being a dying trade as the new 'sticky vinyls' were just emerging, I turned my attention back to the coaches.

I was still too young to be a coach driver, so Tony Patten enrolled me onto the then new government Youth Training Scheme where I was dispatched to the only place in the country that trained PSV mechanics - Tile Hill College in the Midlands. Tony had literally sent me to Coventry! It was good grounding for me, away from home for the first time with other lads from all over the country, from firms now long changed such as Maidstone & District, East Kent, Wilts & Dorset, Eastern National, West Riding, Southern Vectis & Yorkshire Traction.

Vehicles that we worked on at the old depot were such exotica as Daimler Fleetlines, Bristol REs, early Leyland Nationals as well as engines like Gardners, Detroit V8s, and donated Triumphs from the former nearby factories.

After finishing in 1989, I took and passed my PSV test first time in August, driving a 1970 Bedford VAL twin steer, on loan from Cooks in Westfield. I was probably one of the youngest in the area to do so at 18 years of age. My instructor was the very well known Phil Semple who was to later work for Empress.

I had already purchased DHN 455C, the Bedford coach, from Tony while still at school, back in 1986. The test gave me the chance to drive it for the first time and on occasions the firm hired it back for the day. Until then it had been lovingly stored in Githa Road Garage at a very reasonable rent charged by Tony and Harry.

I enjoyed the driving, although I mistakenly changed jobs to work for Cooks in 1990. It eventually turned out on both sides to not be too fruitful and after the bad winter of early 1991, Tony offered me my job back, which I readily accepted. By then I had been forced to sell DHN, a decision I have always later regretted.

I much more appreciated life back with Empress until, in 1995 with Tony's blessing, I decided to have a go on my own and purchased the 'Empress' Leyland Leopard (NKM 133) and started up on 1 April that year as Acclaim Travel. Starting from scratch with very little work and few contacts certainly gives you good grounding on how to get repeat bookings. I was very fortunate to gain many loyal customers. Looking back, at 23 years of age with no track record and one ageing coach, it was good of them to give me a chance. I concentrated on private hire and some extended tours, no school contracts were available or tendered for at the time. It was a wonderful time, although it could be hard going as when you're on your own and things go wrong, there is no back up, and being ill was never an option, although the up side was that I visited some fantastic places and met lots of interesting people - places such as the Glastonbury Festival, or taking marching bands to the D Day celebrations in France. There I had Police motorcycle escorts in front of the coach throughout the tour, although I became aware as each day progressed that the Police were 'knocking back' the *Cassis* (a strong alcoholic beverage) at every stop, without any apparent ill effects!

Just one example of when things went wrong was when on tour with a group in Wales I could not stop the emergency door buzzer going off intermittently all week. On return I went to see the now sadly departed Mark Creasy at his workshop in Rye Harbour who on inspection found that the old Leyland had what is known in the trade as broken its back - probably due to the huge amounts of luggage carried. I think at least three body-to-chassis cross members had broken completely, and another two had fractured; you could say it was probably the window glass in the vehicle that was keeping it together! Mark worked flat out for a week, re-aligning the body, cutting all the cross members away, and fitting new ones. No mean feat, he had the job finished just in time for me to go off the following week with another group to Torquay. I shall always be grateful to him for saving the day.

I also remember moments of pleasure. On one tour, I had to negotiate Lynton Hill in Devon, fully loaded of course and with no run at it. For those who know that part of the country, it's a very steep hill out of the village. It must have been one of the few times that I had had to use 1st. (crawler) gear on the old Leyland, and it was also one of the few times that I could say you could actually hear the engine sing to you under load though the exhaust, as we made the slow run up the incline with the engine working steadily but hard. I will always remember two elderly gentlemen walking down the hill putting their hands to their ears and smiling to me as if to say - that sounds good!

After two years with many miles to varied destinations across the UK & Continent on the clock the faithful Leyland Leopard was traded in for a newer (1983) Leyland Tiger (USV 672) that was originally new to Maidstone & District in Hastings as FKL 172Y.

My father Brian had taken redundancy from the local Gas Board after over 30 years service and had passed his PSV driving test, so made an excellent second driver - he doesn't thrash or over-rev a vehicle!

Although the Tiger was an excellent coach, by the end of the 1997 season it was getting expensive to maintain, and combined with no facilities of my own, diesel costs rising above 49.9p per litre, I decided it was a good time to sell up whilst still ahead of the game.

Tony again offered me to come back as a Mechanic/Driver just before his retirement and the sale of Empress to Jan Auer; after the sale Dad also joined as a driver and from there it's all in the book!

48A "Evening cleaning' Stephen Dine, St Margarets Road Depot. Summer 1985.

48B Acclaim Travel Leyland Leopard NKM 133, at Battersea. 1995 (Paul Green)

Sylvia Turner and her late son Andrew

I became a coach escort back in 1972 for the Grace Eyre Foundation, known locally as the Guardianship Society in the Hastings area. To start with it was a throughout the year contract to take mainly mentally handicapped ladies from local pick ups to a day centre at Calvert Church Hall, which was later changed to the then new West Hill Centre in Bembrook Road in Hastings.

My son Andrew would come along on the run in the coach with me and became interested in Empress early on. He loved getting involved with everything to do with the coaches and I joked that Andrew spent more time at the garage than at home! In the school holiday times - as in the early years the run continued when the schools broke up - Andrew would come round on the run and then go down to the garage for the day to help out. Sometimes he would come home covered from head to toe in oil and grease - quite happy. He would never drink tea at home but did for the first time down at the garage. I also helped out at Tony's home with bookkeeping and statistics etc. until he married Judy in 1976.

Memories of Andrew, by Tony Patten

As I remember, when Sylvia started as a coach escort, Andrew came along, and on the second day he turned up he had produced a home-made coach driver's badge and from there on he was "in with coaches".

Andrew came on trips when it was possible, I remember one where I had dropped a party off in Dover to catch a ferry to France and then had to go back in the evening to bring them home. Andrew came along and we hadn't even left the Dover area before the customers were asking for the first pub stop. We should have been back early evening although we couldn't get them out of the pub till closing time so I was panicking as I knew Andrew should have been back home. Andrew's parents didn't have a phone at home at the time and poor Ken his father was pacing up and down the road (they lived off the A259 en route) as time went on not knowing what to do - before we eventually passed through.

On another occasion, he came with me up to Aylesford Priory near Maidstone in the Bedford VAL six-wheeler. After the passengers had disembarked I let Andrew have a go driving the coach in the large adjacent field as he was already grasping the skills involved in handling a coach. He spent the good part of the day enjoying the experience, although after that I seemed in the forthcoming months to be regularly replacing broken springs on the vehicle!

Up at Githa Road garage we were still using the original hand-wound fuel pump to fill the vehicles up with diesel. The Bedford six wheeler had a large seventy gallon fuel tank, and one occasion it needed refilling when nearly empty. Andrew wanted to fill it up, which had to be done in a cycle of so many turns clockwise followed at the handles stop by the same in reverse order, which was quite tiring even if you have fairly strong arms. Andrew with grim determination would not give up on filling the tank even though his arms must have been dropping off!

Sadly, Andrew was killed by a motorist when out on his bicycle in Harold Road near to the depot in the July of 1976, aged only fifteen years.

Appendix II: Empress Coaches: Bus Services operated and ticket systems

HELLINGLY HOSPITAL: Although usually regarded as an Express Service, this was in fact licenced as an Excursion under the 1930 Road Traffic Act, and a similar licence from Hastings was held by Maidstone & District Motor Services Ltd., at least in postwar years and probably from the 1930s. Empress operations appear to have started with the first coach in 1929 as a private trip for family and invited friends, but was added to the Excursions & Tours licence during the 1930s. Pick-up points were Ore and Harold Place every Wednesday and Sunday afternoon, and by 1960 also at Sidley Station on the first Sunday in the month. Days of operation varied over the years, but Empress last operated the excursion on 18 December 1983.

CONTRACT HIRES - NOT UNDER LICENCE (in date order of commencement):

SUNDAY CHURCH CONTRACTS for Hastings Salvation Army commenced on 4 June 1972, later shared by Robertson St. Congregational Church, until 25.6.95, taken up by St. Mary Star of the Sea Church from 27.11.94 and ran until 25.5.2008.

HILL HOUSE SCHOOL, RYE: started 6.2.1974, ended 19.7.1991. Normally driven by Harry Phillips.

GLYNE GAP SCHOOL: East Sussex County Council contract taken up from 15 June 1978, previously worked by Pandora Holidays. Still operated.

DEBENHAMS, HASTINGS free shoppers' service at Christmas and some Bank Holidays, operated on Sat. 27.12.80 and Thur. 1.1.81; Easter 17.4.81 and 20.4.81, repeated on 28.12.81, 1.1.82, 9.4.82, 12.4.82, 3.5.82, 27.12.82, 1.1.83, 27.12.83, 2.1.84.

SUSSMANS FACTORY, Parker Road: Friday lunchtimes only, started 30.10.1981, ended 24.4.1992.

PESTALOZZI VILLAGE, Sedlescombe, to West St. Leonards School, Mon.-Fri. term time, started 4.9.1990, ended 25.7.1995.

OSBORNE HOUSE, THE RIDGE: (Fridays only): 23.6.1978, ended 4.8.2000.

BROOMHAM SCHOOL, GUESTLING: routes BS1 and BS2, taken up 5.1.1998 on merging with Blackbridge Ltd, continued by Empress until 2.6.2000 (BS1) and 6.7.2000 (BS2).

TORFIELD SCHOOL: started 2.11.1998, ongoing. From 10.9.2007 worked by same coach as Hastings College contract.

WEST ST. LEONARDS & FILSHAM VALLEY SCHOOLS: started 3.12.2001, ongoing.

CLAVERHAM SCHOOL, BATTLE from Westfield, comm.- 9.2003, ended 20.10.06.

HASTINGS COLLEGE, St. Saviours Road annexe, started 14.9.2006, ongoing. From 10.9.2007 worked by same coach as Torfield School.

SERVICES OPERATED UNDER LICENCE *(Minor variations of route are not noted)*

SERVICE EC1 [service 1 in ESCC timetable] for BUSS FARM-FRESH FOODS, Ponswood Estate, commenced as hire contract 3.5.1983, ceased 24.4.92. Became commercial service EC1 from 27.4.92, on a circular route covering much of Hastings and Ore, one journey each way M-F. Route revised 9.10.1995, Operated by Blackbridge Ltd. 5.1.98 to 23.1.98, then Empress Coaches Ltd. Ceased 22.6.98. Deregistered 23.6.98.

SERVICE 303 already operated by Bexhill Bus Co. (1 journey each way M-F): from 13.3.1995 several additional journeys provided by Empress, between Little Common - Bexhill - Sidley - Harley Shute - Harrow Lane - Conquest Hospital. From 27.5.96 joint with Renown, by 6.10.96 reduced to two journeys each way M/W/F, solely worked by Renown.

Increased service M-F restored 28.9.1998, from Bexhill and not serving Little Common. Empress Coaches Ltd. now providing one late afternoon journey each way. From 18 Jan. 1999 service again extended back to Little Common. By 2 June 2002 Empress last journey extended to start from Helenswood Upper and Lower Schools at 1700 during term time. Empress registration cancelled from 28.10.2002, again worked by Renown only.

SERVICES 330-334, EAST SUSSEX COUNTY COUNCIL MOBILITY LINKS: commenced 13.3.1995, M-F, each route one day per week by different routes, with three return journeys from the Town Hall to Conquest Hospital including Dial-A Ride.

330 Mondays: Hastings – Harley Shute – Hollington – Conquest.

331 Tuesdays: Hastings – Old Town – Ore – Conquest.

332 Wednesdays: Hastings – St. Helens Road – Conquest.

333 Thursdays: Hastings – Malvern Way – Conquest.

334 Fridays: Hastings – Filsham Road – Silverhill – Conquest.

Discontinued 4.10.1996 except 331, deregistered 1.1.98 by Patten, service worked by Blackbridge Ltd. (2?), 9, 16 and 23 1.98, then Empress Coaches Ltd. Last operated 23.6.1998. Deregistered 24.6.98.

SERVICE 335 commenced 28.9.1998, five journeys, Conquest Hospital via Elphinstone Road, Hastings Station,- Priory Avenue - Station returning to Conquest Hospital. By 1.7.2000 rerouted and combined with 346 jointly with Coastal, via Upper Church Road - Amherst Road - Station - Baldslow Road - Ore - Pett. Renumbered 347 from 27.10.03. Last operated 20.8.04, covered by Coastal from 23.8.04 and licence transferred 31.8.04

ICKLESHAM VILLAGE BEER FESTIVAL: short-term licence 25-28 July 2002 (operated 25-27th but late journey finished on 28th) Hastings Station - Old Town –Icklesham (Robin Hood), and Rye Station - Rye Harbour - Icklesham.

Repeated 24-26(27) July 2003. Flat fare.

SERVICE 320: commenced 2.11.2002. Saturdays only, Battle Abbey via Battle Station –Sedlescombe - Bodiam Castle – Robertsbridge Station. Last operated and deregistered 26.10.03. (previously operated by Autopoint, Eastbourne Buses and others in various seasons.)

TICKET SYSTEMS:

EXCURSION TICKETS:

Pre-war, white paper tickets in booklets, approx 4" square, titled EMPRESS SALOON COACHES – although the sole vehicle was not a saloon but hooded. Showed seating plan of the Dennis DY 5849 **[49]**.

By 1970s, blue paper, in booklets, 4¾ x 4", with seating plan of 41 seater Bedford SBs.**[50]**

c1980, red on white, for 53 seater **[51]**

ALMEX untitled machines acquired for bus services from 1992, still held in reserve.

WAYFARER MK.1 machines later sold to Renown after bus working ceased in 1994. (no examples known to have survived).

(Illustrations on page 73)

Appendix III: The First Motor Coach

Records of Dennis Bros. Ltd. of Guildford show that chassis no. 70558 left the production line on 4 June 1929, to order of H. Phillips. It is virtually certain that Dennis Bros. also built the motor coach body. Witnesses recall that it was collected from the Works late in July, and driven to Hastings by Stephen Bailey of Coghurst Motor & Coach Body Works, 107 The Ridge, Hastings. Later he rebuilt the body, and is also known to have carried out work for other local bus operators up to the 1950s.

The coach was registered DY 5849 by Hastings Borough Council on Saturday 31 August 1929, and placed in service on the same day. The reason for Harry Phillips' choice of a Dennis is not known, though several of this make, in addition to a variety of others, were in use by contemporary local firms. The chassis was model GL [G type lengthened], with a wheelbase of 12 feet 4 inches compared with six inches less in the standard G type. The additional space was probably used to provide slightly more space between seats, as there is no discernible difference when photographs are compared with the Dennis sales prospectus for the G type. The low floorline needed only one step. Vacuum brakes and pneumatic tyres were standard. The engine was 4 cylinder side valve.

The G type was marketed with a choice of body: a 20 seater bus with fixed roof, or the "all-weather coach". The latter had a roll-back canvas hood, and side windows of frameless glass which dropped down from a fixed wooden frame into the body sides. There were three pairs of seats either side of a central gangway, with a bench of three seats behind them placed centrally to avoid the awkward rear wheel arches, and four seats across the back. A single seat, much coveted by passengers, was placed alongside the driver, and it appears from the seating plan set out on excursion tickets that some sort of seat was provided for a conductor on the driver's right side, though this would be of dubious legality under construction and use regulations. A conductor or other assistance was necessary when the hood needed to be pulled up or down. Hinged doors opening outward were provided at front and back, and an offside door for the driver.

Body framing was of ash, reinforced with steel plates for rigidity, with panels of aluminium and steel. Seats had forged steel legs and spring steel backs, upholstered with leather cushions and backs, and moquette behind the backs. Chassis weight was 1 ton 17 cwt, and the body 15 cwt; the total estimated gross weight with full passenger load was just under four tons. The basic price for the G model was £450 for the chassis and £350 for the coach body – a total of £800. Coaches were advertised as supplied fully painted and varnished to customer's choice of colour; the original livery is believed from one photo **[6]** to have been an all-over light tone. Another early view exists **[52]** which has been hand-coloured, the lower panels light blue but with the addition of a dark blue waist-rail; this is not probably authentic. Other views appear to indicate a considerably darker colour for the panels, but allowance has to be made for the varying tones produced by different types of film.

All surviving photos are from a similar aspect and show the nearside and in some cases the front; no fleet name or owner's name appears in early views, but if the coach was called "The Empress" from the outset, this could have appeared on the rear panel, and the legal lettering required under the 1930 Road Traffic Act was often shown on the offside at this date.

Photos show two modifications at different dates. Early views **[6, 52]** show the seat backs standing prominently six or more inches above the waist-rail, but a year or two later they are much lower and barely visible **[53a, b, c, 54]**.

One winter, probably 1933-4, the coach was rebuilt and modified locally by Bailey's Coach Works, resulting in the addition of a framework of rails above the sides to support the hood, perhaps making it easier to erect from inside without assistance. At this point "The Empress" was sign-written in cursive script boldly along the nearside, and it is possible that the more familiar later livery of maroon and cream first recorded in 1949 was adopted at this time. **[Photo on p iii]**.

Withdrawn c1939/40, reported by October 1941 to be working for Mountain Transport Ltd. London W1, probably on war contracts.

52

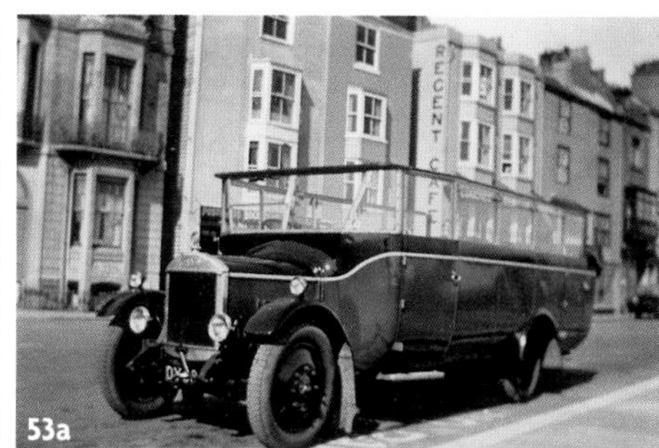
53a

53b

53c

52 DY 5849, the first Dennis showing the original high seat backs – a hand-tinted photo, but the colours are not thought to be authentic. Location: Robertson Terrace, Hastings.

53 (a), (b), (c): DY 5849 Dennis, three views probably taken on one day in the early 1930s, at Caroline Place Stand, Hastings, opposite the "Royal Oak". The seat backs are now much lower.

Appendix IV: Empress Coaches Fleet List

Fleet No	Registration	Make/Model	Chassis No	Body Type	Capacity	First Registration	Bought	Sold
	DY 5849	Dennis GL	70558	Dennis	C20D	31/08/29	(New)	by 10/41
	CKF 783	Bedford WTB	111104	Wilmott	C26R	3/37	by /40	6/60
1.	EDY 44	Bedford OB	127381	Plaxton	C29F	20/02/50	(New)	1/72
2.	BEN 301	Bedford SB3	10070	Duple Vega	C35F	7/52	5/60	8/71
3.	EJK 350	Bedford SB3	60925	Duple Super Vega	C41F	25/03/58	9/67	8/72
4.	6666 AH	Bedford SB1	70370	Duple Vega	C41F	6 /59	10/71	9/74
5.	XBK 576	Bedford SB5	86268	Duple Super Vega	C41F	5/61	8/72	7/76
6.	GPC 58C	Bedford VAL	141612	Plaxton VAL	C52F	1/65	5/73	2/76
7.	NDK 653G	Ford Transit BCO	55JJ49317	Deansgate	12F	/69	10/73	5/77
8.	DHN 455C	Bedford VAS 1	1/1921	Plaxton Embassy	C33F	06/04/65	12/02/74	02/01/87
9.	GGX 556C	Austin FX 4	-	Taxi	-	/65	05/74	30/09/79
10.	MPE 777P	Bedford CF	FY609610	Robin Hood	12F	01/05/76	(New)	8/77
11.	KRL 905L	Bedford NJM	CW451425	Duple Vega 31	C41F	11/07/73	7/76	2/80
12.	RDY 512S	Ford Transit	BDO5SS55894	William Deansgate	12	01/09/77	(New)	11/12/84
13.	SYO 666F	Austin FX4	-	Taxi	-	01/11/67	04/02/78	9/79
14.	RPM 407G	Ford Transit	BCO5HE51095	Ford / South Hants	12	28/11/68	19/06/78	28/01/82
15.	KNK 357G	Bedford VAS 5	9T467965	Duple Vista 25	C29F	10/06/69	09/05/79	13/03/82
16.	SDY 249L	Bedford HA	-	Van	-	/73	25/07/79	09/08/81
17.	VAL 965L	Bedford YRT	CW456151	Plaxton Elite Express	C53F	12/06/73	08/02/80	12/02/86
18.	AKT 949V	Bedford CF	JY622328	Dormobile	C16F	01/07/80	01/11/80	11/03/91
19.	RLR 28L	Bedford PJK	CW453383	Plaxton Elite	C29F	01/06/73	17/07/81	02/12/82
20.	TJK 616S	Bedford HA	92370HY710244	Van	-	15/06/78	08/08/81	01/08/88
21.	ODJ 52R	Bedford NJM	NJM2BZOFW454146	Plaxton Supreme	C41F	01/08/76	02/05/82	16/06/85
22.	JHC 178Y	Bedford PJK	PJK1B2CT103237	Duple Dominant	C29F	01/01/83	03/01/83	01/09/88
23.	B175 LMY	Ford Transit	SFAPXXBDUPDU23185	Mellor	C16F	11/12/84	(New)	25/10/93
24.	JEC 407T	Ford Transit	BDVPUR253520	Dormobile	C16F	01/03/79	01/05/85	09/89
25.	MCD 795W	Ford Transit	BDVPAD473180	Dormobile	C14F	01/04/81	12/08/85	01/87
26.	URO 921E	Bedford VAM	VAM146872727	Plaxton Panorama	C45F	13/06/67	24/04/86	23/08/86
27.	JRM 800L	Bedford PJK	PJK1B202T472788	Duple Vista	C29F	08/02/73	19/05/86	27/10/86
28.	MAX 331X	Bedford PJK	PJK1BZOLW451524	Plaxton Supreme	C29F	01/02/82	23/01/87	01/09/92
29.	D713 HUA	Freight Rover	SAZZMZFC78N256762	Optare	B16F	08/09/86	14/08/87	14/08/93
30.	GDY 124X	Honda Acty	-	Pick up	-	01/04/82	05/08/88	09/07/90
31.	NKM 133	Leyland Leopard	PSU3E/4R7802671	Plaxton Supreme	C53F	01/09/78	01/09/88	31/03/95
32.	200 FXM	Ford Transit	BDVPDC85814	Dormobile	C16F	01/12/83	07/08/89	18/11/90
33.	JLN 237N	Bristol LHS	LHS207	Plaxton Supreme	C35F	01/05/75	07/10/89	2/92
34.	EHC 844W	Honda Acty	-	Van	-	25/05/81	25/05/90	13/07/90
35.	E319 VKR	Bedford Rascal	-	Pick up	-	25/01/88	20/06/90	05/01/98
36.	H389 KPY	CVE	SDKPSZFPKFWD00152	Omni	C21F	06/09/90	(New)	
37.	H390 KPY	CVE	SDKPSZFPKFWS00153	Omni	C21F	01/09/90	(New)	05/12/05
38.	A843 XFW	Bedford YMP	SKFYMP2D2ET103579	Plaxton Paramount	C41F	01/05/84	05/10/91	28/03/02
39.	B157 FWJ	Bedford PJK	SKFPJK182FT106618	Plaxton Supreme IV	C27F	03/05/85	27/02/92	30/04/98
40.	F486 XON	Freight Rover	SAZZMERC7AN834362	Carlyle	C16F	24/11/88	31/08/93	21/07/01
41.	J397 KOR	Renault Master	VF1FB30ASO3499078	Jubilee	C15F	04/07/92	20/10/93	06/09/01
42.	FIL 8605	Bedford YMP	SKFYMP2DZ|GT103752	Plaxton Paramount	C38F	18/04/86	21/02/95	03/09/99
43.	IIL 6765	Ford R1114	BCRSWD412310	Plaxton Supreme IV	C53F	13/06/80	03/07/95	27/07/95
44.	J996 MKM	OBC Omni	SDLPSZFPKFWD00306	Omni	DP20F	29/10/91	14/07/95	21/07/04

Fleet No	Registration	Make/Model	Chassis No	Body Type	Capacity	First Registration	Bought	Sold
45.	CBM 12X	Leyland Tiger TRCTL	8101289	Plaxton Supreme VI GT	C53F	01/05/82	05/01/98	18/05/98
46.	H165 OHK	Ford Transit	SFAVXXBDVVLP16109	Red Kite Conversion	C14F	09/05/91	05/01/98	4/00
47.	F572 HUF	Ford Transit	SFAZXXBDVZJD63771	Ford	C14F	13/09/88	05/01/98	1/00
48.	K885 BRW	Toyota Coaster	HDB300001860	Caetano Optimo II	C21F	07/09/92	30/04/98	18/09/99
49.	LIL 5292	DAF SB2300DHTD	245251	Plaxton Paramount3200	C53F	02/04/84	18/05/98	23/09/99
50.	L760 SDY	Ford Transit	SFAAXXBDVAPM67560	Dormobile	C20F	02/08/93	03/09/99	11/05/05
51.	EBM 460T	Bedford YMT	YMT3DZ0JW452327	Plaxton Supreme IV	C53F	31/05/79	16/02/00	12/10/00
52.	E768 HCD	Ford Transit	SFAVXXBDVVHC62284	Dormobile	DP20F	19/10/87	14/04/00	07/11/00
53.	DBB 127V	Bedford	YLQ/S YLQ2DZOKW450767	Plaxton Supreme IV	C35F	09/06/80	29/06/00	01/02 (withdrawn 08/01)
54.	D77 HRU	Bedford YNT	SKFYNT3NZHT100827	Plaxton Paramount 3	C53F	01/05/87	12/10/00	25/09/03
55.	L408 ORC	Iveco 49.10	ZCF04970005001734	Factory Conversion	C19F	17/06/94	4/01?	08/04/02
56.	D36 ALR	Bedford YMP	SKFYMP2DZGT103475	Plaxton Paramount 2	C41F	01/08/86	24/06/01	14/02/03
57.	M965 RKJ	Ford Transit	SFADXXBDVDRJ50098	Devon Conversion Exe	DP16FL	27/02/95	28/11/01	16/11/06
58.	J430 WFA	Mercedes-Benz 709	6690032N001301	Plaxton Beaver	C25F	26/06/92	08/04/02	12/09/06
59.	NEC 237K	Bedford VAL 70	2T472884	Plaxton Panorama EliteII	C53F	01/04/72	11/06/02	14/02/03
60.	M351 TDO	Mercedes-Benz 814	WDB6703132NO23917	Autobus Classique	C33F	01/09/94	14/02/03	23/01/06
61.	K297 UKR	OBC Omni	SDNP5ZFPKFWD00370	Omni	DP20F	04/05/93	14/02/03	28/02/04
62.	HBZ 4673	Mercedes-Benz	0303 30039523048222	Mercedes Benz	C53F	14/04/87	25/09/03	15/10/04
63.	N183 WMS	Ford Tourneo	SFAFXXBDVFSP56884	Ford	-8-	26/01/96	10/06/04	26/08/06
64.	R46 JUB	Ford Transit	WFOAXXBDVATE02311	Devcoplan	DP16FL	02/02/98	24/06/04	21/05/09
65.	T361 AFG	Ford Transit	WFOAXXBDVAXCO5481	Chassis Developments	C16F	02/08/99	12/07/04	
66.	L317 YDU	Mercedes-Benz 709	WDB6690032N021476	Alexander Sprint	C25F	10/06/94	04/01/05	02/05/07
67.	P639 ROU	Iveco 59.12	ZCFC5980102192164	Bedwas	DP25FL	30/08/96	30/06/05	17/02/09
68.	R128 AWF	Mercedes-Benz 614	WDB6683222N072307	Devon	DP16FL	06/07/98	05/07/05	
69.	GAZ 1066	Dennis Javelin	10SDA2156/1306	W S Vanguard 2	C41F	01/09/95	07/09/05	15/10/07
70.	N36 PDF	Iveco 59.12	ZCFC5980002165948	Bedwas	DP24FL	26/06/96	16/02/06	10/12/07
71.	YR02 YTH	Optare Alero	Z1000000000238	Optare	DP16F	25/03/02	16/11/06	16/01/08
72.	YR02 YTG	Optare Alero	Z1000000000237	Optare	DP16F	25/03/02	29/11/06	17/01/08
73.	T713 YDV	Toyota Coaster	TW043BB5000001317	Caetano Optimo IV	C26F	01/05/99	16/03/07	25/07/08
74.	T174 BVV	Ford Transit	WFOAXXBDVAVG77624	Chassis Developments	DP15FL	13/04/99	15/11/07	
75.	V403 BNH	Ford Transit	WFOAXXBDVAXC07070	Chassis Developments	DP15FL	02/12/99	15/11/07	
76.	XPT 454F	Bedford CA	7V801413	Martin Walter Utilabus	C11F	17/11/67	30/01/08	19/04/09
77.	V7 PCC	Mercedes Benz 814	WDB6703742N083356	Autobus Nouvelle 2	C29F	13/10/99	12/03/08	
78.	V74 GKH	Mercedes Benz Vito	VSA63809423232642	Alphatec (npcv)	-8-	11/11/99	16/04/08	24/10/09
79.	WV51 ZZG	Citroen Dispatch	VF7BZWJZA12842347	special conversion (npcv)	-2-	11/09/01	11/07/08	
80.	R16 CTC	Mercedes Benz Sprinter	WDB9046632R223775	Optare Ferqui Soroco	C16F	26/09/01	14/11/08	
81.	Y797 OFE	Mercedes Benz Sprinter	WDB9046632R163546	Optare Ferqui Soroco	C16F	07/03/01	30/03/09	
82.	S577ACT	Mercedes Benz 814	WDB6703742N074175	Autobus Nouvelle	C29F	23/09/98	09/04/09	
83.	T243 MHK	Mercedes Benz Vito	VSA63806423166809		-7-	01/03/99	15/09/09	30/10/09

Notes :
Fleet numbering began when the business was purchased by Tony Patten in July 1971
05/01/98 Business sold to Jan Auer on fleet number 44.
20/12/99 Business sold to Stephen Dine on fleet number 49.
39. B157 FWJ sold to Blackbridge Travel on 17/09/97 re-joining the fleet on 05/01/98 again as Fleet No 39, and was part exchanged for fleet no. 48.
43. IIL 6765 taken back to Bob Vale (Dealer) for re-sale after short use as a replacement coach for summer
78 & 79 are operated as non pcv vehicles.
79 & 83. Both Mercedes Vitos are 108 Models.
80 & 81. Both Mercedes Sprinters are 413 CDI models.
77 & 82 Both Mercedes are 0814 Vario models.
78. Withdrawn on 15/09/09.
Fleet Numbers 57, 64, 67, 68, 70, 74 & 75 are equipped with external cassette type wheelchair lifts, seating plans can differ from maximum seating capacity shown depending on wheelchair space required.
Not listed is CVE Omni G685 VYN (Chassis No 00190, new 1990, DP20F) that was owned but not operated by Empress. Purchased for spares from R S Dosanjh, Strood who acquired it from Kent County Council in 5/97. Dosanjh withdrew vehicle by 4/00 but re-instated by 4/01. Withdrawn again by 5/02 until sale to Empress by /03. Scrapped by Saunters, Three Oaks in 2003.

Known previous owners

	DY 5849	New.
	CKF 783	New to Barkers Motors Ltd, 224 Smithdown Road, Wavertree, Liverpool (as C25R) then Empress.
1.	EDY 44	New.
2.	BEN 301	New to Auty's Tours, Bury, Lancs; Tremain, Zelah, Cornwall 8/55; then Empress.
3.	EJK 350	New to Jackson, Eastbourne (16) then Empress.
4.	6666 AH	New to Babbage, Cromer; -?-; Walsh, Hemel Hempstead; then Empress via Yeates (dealer).
5.	XBK 576	New to Byng, Portsmouth by 5/61 in their Royal Blue fleet; Darch & Wilcox, Martock, Somerset 10/61; -?- ; Woburn, London WC1; Waterhouse, Polegate 1/68; then Empress.
6.	GPC 58C	New to Cooke, Stoughton, Guildford; passed with business to Safeguard, Guildford -/66; Bodman, Worton, Devizes 4/68; Rambler Coaches, Hastings 4/73; then Empress.
7.	NDK 653G	New as a non-psv to A. Henshaw, Rye, became PSV 10/71; acquired with business by G & C A Trill (Graham's Coaches) Rye 10/72 sold 11/73; then Empress.
8.	DHN 455C	New to Alpha, Brighton; -?- Parnaby (Ruxley Coaches), Tolworth; Waterhouse, Polegate 12/70; then Empress.
9.	GGX 556C	New to ?; Thomas Taxis, Hastings; then Empress.
10.	MPE 777P	New (supplied by Robin Hood conversions).
11.	KRL 905L	New to R K & R E Webber (Webber Bros) Blisland, Bodmin, Cornwall; -?-; Lloyd, Melling, Lancs; then Empress via Kirkbys (dealer).
12.	RDY 512S	New (supplied by Hollingsworths, Hastings).
13.	SYO 666F	New to ? ; Private Owner (care home), Hastings; then Empress.
14.	RPM 407G	New to W B Thomsett, (Cooks Coaches) Westfield; then Empress.
15.	KNK 357G	New to Comex 3 (see notes); -?-; O. Porter, Dummer, Basingstoke, Hants (acquired after 1/73); Lock, London SE8 12/76; -?-; Shaw, Warwick 3/78; then Empress via Bakers (dealer).
16.	SDY 249L	New to ? ; Coombs Motors, Hastings; then Empress.
17.	VAL 965L	New to Barton, Chilwell (1252); then Empress via Kirkbys (dealer).
18.	AKT 949V	New as Dormobile demonstrator; then Empress.
19.	RLR 28L	New to Neale, Hampton, London; Hilldrup, (Gemini) Great Canfield, Essex 4/78; then Empress.
20.	TJK 616S	New to ? ; Coombs Motors, Hastings (dealer); then Empress.
21.	ODJ 52R	New to Barry Cooper, Stockton Heath, Warrington, Cheshire; then Empress via Lancashire Motor Traders (dealer).
22.	JHC 178Y	New, supplied by Kirkby (dealer).
23.	B175 LMY	New, supplied by Crystals, Orpington (dealer).
24.	JEC 407T	New to Tuers, Morland, Cumbria; Casson, Workington 5/81; then Empress via Crystals (dealer).
25.	MCD 795W	New to Airport Parking, Copthorne; then Empress.
26.	URO 921E	New to Parnaby (Ruxley Coaches) Tolworth; C D Smith, Brenzett 11/71; G & C A Trill (Grahams Coaches) Rye 2/81; then Empress.
27.	JRM 800L	New to Messengers of Aspatria, Cumberland; W G Norris Haulage (Norris Coaches), Rochester 7/74 sold by /79; -?-; Whent, Mayland,Essex 7/79; then Empress via Kirkbys (dealer).
28.	MAX 331X	New to Thomas, Clydach Vale, Mid Glamorgan, Wales; Rambler, Hastings (31) 6/86; then Empress.
29.	D713 HUA	New to Yorkshire Rider (1713); then Empress via Mosley (dealer).
30.	GDY 124X	New to ? ; Car Auctions, Brett Drive, Bexhill; then Empress.
31.	NKM 133	New to Midland Red (727) as C46F; then Shamrock & Rambler, Bournemouth (133) 6/85; then Empress via Stuart Johnson (dealer).
32.	200 FXM	New to Haines Hire, Sidcup; then Empress.
33.	JLN 237N	New to F G Wilder (Golden Miller) Feltham; Cresswells, Church Gresley, Derbyshire 5/78; UKAEA, Winfrith, Dorset 9/79; Davies, Bridport, Dorset 2/89; then Empress.
34.	EHC 844W	New to ? ; Private Owner, Hastings; then Empress.
35.	E319 VKR	New to ? ; Dealer, Hastings; then Empress.
36.	H389 KPY	New.
37.	H390 KPY	New.
38.	A843 XFW	New to Hornsby, Ashby, Lincolnshire; then Empress.
39.	B157 FWJ	New to Glynglen (Tristar), Heathrow; taken over by Capital, West Drayton; then Empress via Bob Vale (dealer).
40.	F486 XON	New to Stanford in the Vale Community Bus, Hatford, Oxfordshire; then Empress via Jubilee, Midlands (dealer).

41. J397 KOR — Renault UK, Southampton; converted by Jubilee, Midlands as demonstrator, fitted with 8 leather seats (dealer/ converter); then Empress.
42. FIL 8605 — New to Armchair, Brentford; Bammants, Fakenham 4/91; Sanders, Holt 2/92; Chivers, Wallington 2/94; then Empress.
43. IIL 6765 — New to North, Smallfield, Surrey; -?-; Cuttings, Brockley 8/84; Hyltone, High Wycombe 2/91; then Empress via Bob Vale (dealer).
44. J996 MKM — New to Kent County Council; operated by Fuggles, Benenden on Kent Karrier Services by 6/92; later Wealden PSV, Five Oak Green; then S L Edgecombe (Airport Shuttle/Mercury) Hoo, Kent; then Empress via dealer in Heathrow area.
45. CBM 12X — New to Premier Albanian, Watford; Blackbridge, Guestling /97; then Empress.
46. F572 HUF — New to ? ; Blackbridge, Guestling; then Empress.
47. H165 OHK — New to ? ; Blackbridge Guestling; then Empress.
48. K885 BRW — New to Bonas (Supreme Coaches), Coventry; then Hallmark, Luton 11/94; then Empress via S J Carlton (dealer).
49. LIL 5292 — New to Sharrock & Littler, Westhoughton, Greater Manchester; -?-; Browne, East Grinstead (3); then Empress.
50. L760 SDY — New to Bexhill Community Bus, Bexhill; then Empress.
51. EBM 460T — New to Scotland & Bates, Appledore, Kent; then Empress.
52. E768 HCD — New as a Dormobile demonstrator, (registered E863 UKO); B P & J Rodemark (Autopoint) Herstmonceux 2/91, reregistered 1241 AP in 10/95; then Empress.
53. DBB 127V — New to Armchair, Brentford; Spirit of London; -?-; Consett Bus & Coach Co., (7) Consett; then Empress via Yeates (dealer).
54. D77 HRU — New to Buckland, Hurst; -?-; W H Fowler & Sons, Holbeach Drove; then Empress.
55. L408 ORC — New to Brooklyn Coaches, Shirland, Alfreton, Derbyshire; then Empress.
56. D36 ALR — New to Capital, West Drayton; -?-; Evans, Tregaron; then Empress.
57. M965 RKJ — New to Kent County Council; on hire to Community Transport for the Newhaven area, (npsv) Lewes; then Empress via H W Pickrell, Essex (dealer).
58. J430 WFA — New to PMT (MMM 430) with subsidiary Turners; then Empress via Houston Ramm (dealer).
59. NEC 237K — New to Brown, Ambleside; Browne, Brabourne 10/76; Thomsett, Deal 11/82; (still owned 5/96, sold by 5/98) -?-; Abbeyways, Halifax; then Paul Emery, Val's Classic Coaches (dealer) then Empress.
60. M351 TDO — New to Pemico, Bermondsey, London; Dawson (GPD), Heywood, Lancs; then Empress via Houston Ramm, Rochdale (dealer).
61. K297 UKR — New to Kent County Council; Swanage Taxis, Dorset; then Empress via Houston Ramm, Rochdale (dealer).
62. HBZ 4673 — New to Hirst, Holmfirth as C49FT; Redwing, London ; -?-; R N Lyles, Mirfield, West Yorkshire; then Empress.
63. N183 WMS — New to ? Parkhurst Taxis, Bexhill; then Empress.
64. R46 JUB — New to Wakefield Metropolitan District Council, West Yorkshire (3046) (npsv); then Empress via Heatons, Wigan (Dealer).
65. T361 AFG — New to Bexhill Community Bus; then Empress.
66. L317 YDU — New 10/6/94 to Midland Red (South) Rugby, Warwickshire; Hampshire Bus, Chichester 9/12/01 (807), based at Andover, painted into group standard livery 6/2/02, re numbered 40117 6/1/03, transferred to Southdown Motor Services, Chichester 31/7/03 as ancillary vehicle. Controllers office at Havant Bus depot, then re allocated for disposal 19/9/04; then Empress.
67. P639 ROU — New to London Borough of Wandsworth (4423); then to Chelmsford Commercials 6/05 (dealer); then Empress.
68. R128 AWF — New to Doncaster Health Care Trust; Raicha, Leicester 4/04; Taxico (Goldstraw) (3), Leek 4/5/04; then Mike Halford Coaches, Bridport, Dorset (dealer); then Empress.
69. GAZ 1066 — New to Royal Air Force, carrying military registration ER 75 AA and based, for at least part of its life, at Brize Norton; then Empress via Witham SV, MOD Disposals, Grantham.
70. N36 PDF — New to ? ; Wilkinson (Heritage Travel), Cinderford, Gloucestershire; then Empress.
71. YR02 YTH — New to East Sussex C C to Rye Community Transport by8/02; then Empress.
72. YR02 YTG — New to East Sussex C C to Rye Community Transport by 3/03; then Empress.
73. T713 YDV — New to Mike Halford, Bridport, Dorset; then Empress.
74. T174 BVV — New to Stockton-on-Tees Borough Council, Billingham, Cleveland (npsv) (registered keeper Specialist Fleet Services, Northampton); then Empress.
75. V403 BNH — New to Stockton-on-Tees Borough Council, Billingham, Cleveland (npsv) (registered keeper Specialist Fleet Services, Northampton); then Empress.
76. XPT 454F — New to Sinclair, South Hetton, Durham 17/11/67; A Beck, South Hetton, Durham 11/5/70; Rochester & Marshall, (?) 6/1/71; Fowler, Holbeach Drove 9/72; then ? 11/74 (unknown owners until) Hughes, Ashford, Kent; then unknown owner in Yorkshire; Dick Craven, Sutton-on-the Forest, North Yorkshire, (preservation); then Empress.
77. V7 PCC — New to P C Coaches, Lincoln; J P Minicoaches, Forfar, Angus, Scotland 2/9/07; then Empress.
78. V74 GKH — New to ?; -?-; Acklam, Beverley, East Yorkshire (npcv); Private Owner, Bradford; then Empress.
79. WV51 ZZG — New to Private Owner; then Holloway Commercials, (dealer) 2/10/07; then Empress.
80. R16 CTC — New to Forsey (Floyds), Charmouth, as FX51 BOH; Creative Travel Connections, Broxburn, West Lothian 6/5/05; then Empress.

81. Y797 OFE New to Ferreira (A F Tours), Earlsfield; Team Travel, Crawley 12/04; -?-; Bathpool Minibuses, Taunton 2/3/07; then Empress.
82. S577 ACT New to Thurlby (D & P Coaches), Aldershot; Boultons, Cardington, Shropshire 1/11/01; then Empress.
83. T243 MHK New to -?-; Private owner, St Neots, Cambs then Empress.

Notes.
DY 5849 After the war Mountain Transport was Mountain Transport Services, Manresa Road, Chelsea, London SW3. Manresa Road is off the Kings Road and near to the Royal Brompton and Royal Marsden Hospitals. Between 4/48 and 6/49 Mountain Transport hired nine different vehicles to London Transport for use from Hammersmith, Mortlake and Putney Bridge garages. These nine vehicles were surprisingly of six different makes (TSM, Bedford, Commer, Crossley, Austin and most famously ex-Trent SOS).
2. BEN 301 Auty's Tours also had Bedford SB's AEN 990 (later Tunbridge, Rolvenden), BEN 300/2/3/500/1 and others plus other makes. Auty's Tours went back to 1939 and before that as Auty Brothers, to 1924, possibly earlier as part of Spencer & Auty. The Coach interests of the company were acquired by Ribble in 1/56. Some Ribble vehicles carried Auty's names until 1/60. Auty's continued for a while as a car dealership.
4. 6666 AH Babbage also had an SB1/Duple C41F registered 6666 VF.
8. DHN455C took part in the 1965 Brighton Coach Rally when owned by Alpha.
15. KNK357G was used as part of a fleet of 20 similar coaches on the Comex 3 Overland expeditions when new in 1969. Travelling on a peaceful expedition from England to India and back via Frankfurt, Germany, It carried the Yorkshire contingent. When en route, the coach sustained damage from a boulder rolling down a hillside on the Konak Pass near to Trabzan, jamming the accelerator pedal and necessitating hasty repairs to its nearside front, although it still finished the entire journey, a round trip of over 17,500 miles.
17. VAL965L was one of ten similar vehicles new to Barton in 1973 (VAL963-972L)
19. RLR 28L Neale, Hampton had two Panorama-bodied VAS5s new in 1973, the other was RLR 27L.
31. NKM 133 one of five similar coaches new to Midland Red (with 46 and 49 seats) in 1978 (WOC725-729T)
29. Was one of 15 similar vehicles new to Yorkshire Rider (1701-1715) C701 KBT and D702-715 HUA
45. Premier also owned identical coach CBM 13X, that appeared on the TV series 'The League of Gentlemen'.
48. Bonas (Supreme Coaches) had similar vehicle K886 BRW.
53. Armchair also had MNM26 & 27V all new as C28F.
62. Hirst had D346-8 CBC & D350-358 CBC some as C53F & 352/6/8 as C49FT.
66. Midland Red (South) Rugby also had 307-325 (L307-325 YDU).

Known Subsequent Owners

	DY 5849	Mountain Transport Ltd, London, SW1 by 10/41.
	CKF 783	Crystalate Ltd, Tonbridge (Staff Transport) last licenced 7/64, broken up on site /65.
1.	EDY 44	A.W.Patten, Empress 7/71; Pestalozzi Children's Village Trust, Sedlescombe 1/72; 4th Uckfield Scout Group -/74; M C Ash (Mole Valley Transport Services), Esher, Surrey (later Leatherhead, Surrey) for intended preservation c 1977. Project never finished; unknown owner possibly for preservation.
2.	BEN 301	A.W.Patten, Empress 7/71; E. Ive (dealer) St Leonards 8/71; St Mary's Church of England School, Crawley (npsv) c 12/71, re-registered 827 PPO 6/76; Pickersgill, (dealer) [no location given] 9/76 then mobile caravan by -/78 [location not given]
3.	EJK 350	A.W.Patten, Empress 7/71; Involved in accident. 8/72 Recovered by Cousens, Ninfield, later scrapped at Mount Pleasant Garage, Ninfield, East Sussex.
4.	6666 AH	Warren, Ticehurst; .R.Bishop (Island Travel), South Willesborough, Ashford, Kent 12/74, withdrawn when operation ceased by 11/75.
5.	XBK 576	Kirkbys (dealer) part exchanged for 11.
6.	GPC 58C	Bakers (dealer); Watkins, Brighton 8/76, sold for scrap by 5/78.
7.	NDK 653G	Shippen, Fobbing, Essex 6/77.
8.	DHN 455C	S. Dine, Hastings (preservation) 2/1/87; Mobile home, Newbury /91 (see notes).
9.	GGX 556C	Pestalozzi Children's Village Trust, Sedlescombe.
10.	MPE 777P	Hollingsworths, Hastings (dealer) part exchanged for 12; Thatched House Coaches, London E6; Ian Stockdale, Selby by 9/84, withdrawn 8/86 and subsequently scrapped.
11.	KRL 905L	Kirkbys (dealer); Lewington, Harold Hill, Essex; Carrolls, Collier Row, Essex 6/84.
12.	RDY 512S	Crystals, Orpington (dealer) part exchanged for 23.
13.	SYO 666F	Pestalozzi Childrens Village Trust, Sedlescombe.
14.	RPM 407G	Local owner, Hastings; private owner, Hastings by 3/82.
15.	KNK 357G	Jacksons, London SE20 3/82; Bridport Football Club 8/83; withdrawn 3/84.
16.	SDY 249L	Scrapped.
17.	VAL 965L	Alpha, Brighton (dealer); Imperial, Chislehurst; Jones, Abbey Wood 4/91; Granby Coachworks, Northfleet (dealer) /94.
18.	AKT 949V	Kenilworth Mission, Hastings (npsv).
19.	RLR 28L	G S G Bone (Western Garage), Hove by 3/83; Sleepeezee, London SW 19 (npsv) 6/84; withdrawn 8/90.
20.	TJK 616S	Private owner, Three Oaks (possibly Scrapped).
21.	ODJ 52R	Alpha, Brighton (dealer); W J & M A Roberts, Aylesham, Kent 6/85 sold by 4/87; Pearce, Yatton, Somerset 1/86; Beeline, Warminster 8/88; Ridler, Dulverton 5/90; withdrawn 11/92.
22.	JHC 178Y	Stuart Johnson, (dealer). Part exchanged for 31; Maltby Miners (who were a PSV licensed operator); Flanagan, Grappenhall 4/92; Martleys, Portlaoise, Eire 12/98; reregistered 83-LS-422 2/99; Gorey Coach, Gorey, Eire; Edwards, Enniscorthy, Eire by 3/02; withdrawn 5/02.
23.	B175 LMY	C & R Travel, Gosport; Jennings, Hayling Island 9/95; withdrawn 11/97.
24.	JEC 407T	Scrapped by Empress at Githa Road Garage, Hastings.
25.	MCD 795W	B P & J Rodemark (Autopoint) Herstmonceux; Sluggett, Holsworthy 12/87; withdrawn 9/95; scrapped at AD Coach Sales, Witheridge by 11/99. (may not have been used by Autopoint)
26.	URO 921E	F J Morton, Bexhill 7/86, sold by 5/89; mobile home, Rye Harbour by 3/90.
27.	JRM 800L	Spyway School, St Leonards; hippies caravan by 5/92.
28.	MAX 331X	Bob Vale (dealer); P & S, Hillingdon; Rogers, Navan, Eire 1/94; reregistered 82-MH-493.
29.	D713 HUA	K J Morgan (Bygone), Staplehurst, still owned 5/97, sold by 5/98; derelict at Hams Travel depot, Benenden (still in Bygone livery) 7/05 later scrapped.
30.	GDY 124X	Private Owner, Westfield Lane.
31.	NKM 133	S. Dine, Acclaim Travel, Hastings 3/95; P A Lockhart & P R Gainsbury, Conquest Travel, Hastings 4/97; Wealden PSV (dealer) as HFG 622 T; Fitzpatrick, Listowel, Eire 10/99, became 78-KY-637 in 11/99, withdrawn for scrap 8/04.
32.	200 FXM	Kenhire, Sutton; Rich, Wallington by 1/98; withdrawn by 6/99.
33.	JLN 237N	Bob Vale (dealer); Charter, Dorset; reregistered HIL 7598 4/92; Charlton, Weymouth by 2/93, exported (to ?) 10/98.
34.	EHC 844W	Private Owner, Hastings.
35.	E319 VKR	Retained by A Patten on 05/01/98 out of use 1/12/05,(stored in Moat Lane, Sedlescombe).
36.	H389 KPY	J Auer, Empress 1/98; S. Dine, Empress 12/99.
37.	H390 KPY	Private Owner, London.
38.	A843 XFW	Watsons, Redhill, Surrey.

39. B157 FWJ S J Carlton (dealer), part exchanged for 48, Reed, Kinsley; Barsby, Mansfield Woodhouse 9/98; McEwans, Mansfield 11/00.
40. F486 XON Malta Re-discovered. (Export).
41. J397 KOR PP & RJ Nolloth, Hastings; private owner.
42. FIL 8605 Mike Lewis, Powys, Wales; Neal (R & T Tours), Deal 9/02; reregistered B13 RTT 9/02; reregistered C768 YKK 11/04, exported (to ?) 2/06.
43. IIL 6765 Bob Vale, (dealer) Sold for spares, via Bob Vale.
44. J996 MKM ETS Patient Transport, Swanley, Kent (non-PSV).
45. CBM 12X Sussex Coaches, Horsham.
46. F572 HUF Private owner, St Leonards on Sea.
47. H165 OHK Private owner, St Leonards on Sea.
48. K885 BRW Frank Hilton, Wigan; reregistered 963 FHT 10/99; reregistered K885 BRW by 3/06, withdrawn by 9/07.
49. LIL 5292 Dews, Somersham, scrapped after accident 2003.
50. L760 SDY Potters Bar Coach Hire, Hertfordshire; converted to party bus, then mobile home, Surrey, reregistered TPA 646; reregistered L760 SDY; exported 10/08.
51. EBM 460T Dews, Somersham; Stans of Malden 9/01; Morss, Wingfield 11/05.
52. E768 HCD Craven Arms Taxis & Coaches, withdrawn by 10/04.
53. DBB 127V Private Owner, Hastings; Smith, Longport by 6/02; Evans, Stoke-on-Trent 5/03; Collinson, Ribchester, Lancashire by 12/04; withdrawn by 2/05; Parked in depot (location unknown) /08.
54. D77 HRU Herdmans, Clyro, Powys; Daughton Lixnaw, Eire 9/07, 87-KY-3406 10/07; McCullough, Drogheda, Eire 9/08; Carroll, Drogheda, Eire 2/09.
55. L408 ORC Houston Ramm, (dealer) part exchanged for 58.
56. D36 ALR Houston Ramm, (dealer) along with 59. Part exchanged for 60; McChrystal, Kirkintilloch; Turner, Huyton 8/04; Dodd & Tilley, Haydon Bridge by 10/06; In scrapyard, Rugby /06.
57. M965 RKJ Rye Community Transport (part exchanged for 71 & 72).
58. J430 WFA Clive V Wilson (Mr Clive Travel), Portslade, West Sussex.
59. NEC 237K Houston Ramm, with 56 (dealer) part exchanged for 60; Johnsons Coaches, Worksop (preservation).
60. M351 TDO L J Edwards, Hailsham.
61. K297 UKR ETS Private Ambulance, Swanley, Kent.
62. HBZ 4673 J A Mancini (Kingsman International Travel), Faversham.
63. N183 WMS Snowdrop Travel, Dagenham.
64. R46 JUB Carlone, Wraysbury, Middlesex.
65. T361 AFG
66. L317 YDU Clive V Wilson (Mr Clive Travel), Portslade, West Sussex. Re-registered as DIG 3765 on sale.
67. P639 ROU Raines, South Shields; -?-;
68. R128 AWF
69. GAZ 1066 Ian W Bruce, Aberdeenshire.
70. N36 PDF Filsham Wheelers, Bexhill (private owner); Hastings Area Community Transport, Hastings (non-PSV)
71. YR02 YTH A Limos, Bromley.
72. YR02 YTG Bio Travel, Newquay.
73. T713 YDV Sunnyside Travel, Caterham, Surrey.
74. T174 BVV
75. V403 BNH
76. XPT 454F Private owner, Weston Super Mare (preservation)
77. V7 PCC
78. V74 GKH Dealer, Hubberts Bridge, Boston, Lincs.
79. WV51 ZZG
80. R16 CTC
81. Y797 OFE
82. S577 ACT
83. T243 MHK Rik-Fit, Stirchley, Birmingham

Notes.
8. Sold on for continued preservation. After conversion to a mobile home, DHN455C travelled to Spain, before arriving back in the UK and after time in Hampshire, was reported derelict in Oxford /94.

Registration Transfers

Before the use of 1066 suffix issues beginning with the purchase of JAZ 1066 in May 2000, the registration 200 FXM purchased with fleet no 32 was the only issue subsequently used on fleet no 33 and then 38. Other cherished marks shown on vehicles before 2000, were sold on with the vehicles, except NKM 133, which was loaned to Stephen Dine, Acclaim Travel, still on former fleet no 31, before being retained by Tony Patten, before being re purchased privately by Stephen Dine in 7/09.

31 WOC 727T to NKM 133 in 6/86 and HFG 622T in 8/99 before export to Ireland.
32 A705 NGS to 200 FXM by 6/87 and A498 NJK in 10/90.
33 JLN 237N to 200 FXM in 11/90 and JYJ 146N in 11/91.
36 H389 KPY to CAZ 1066 on 9/02 back to H389 KPY on 15/7/05.
37 H390 KPY to KLZ 1066 on 31/3/03, back to H390 KPY on 15/7/05.
38 A424 SAG to 6053 RH on 5/84 became A843 XFW on 10/91, 200 FXM in 11/91, PAZ 1066 on 13/8/01, to B904 MWV (in error by DVLA) on 7/3/02 then corrected to A51 GAP on 21/3/02.
41 J397 KOR to ELZ 1066 in 11/00
42 C407 DML to FIL 8605 in 9/89
43 JPG 715V to IIL 6765 in 7/93
44 J996 MKM to ELZ 1066 on 4/10/01 (registration sold with vehicle)
49 A572 PCW to LIL 5292 in 12/95
50 L760 SDY to PAZ 1066 on 7/3/02 back to L760 SDY on 29/4/05
52 E863 UKO to 1241 AP in 10/95, E768 HCD in 3/00, JAZ 1066 in 5/00
53 MNM 28V to 697 BYU by 3/86, DBB 127V by 5/96, BHZ 1066 in 10/00
54 D77 HRU to JAZ 1066 in 11/00 and HBZ 4673 (from fleet no 62) on sale.
55 L408 ORC to KIW 1066 on 26/6/01
56 D36 ALR to BHZ 1066 in 8/01 back to D36 ALR on 25/5/03
57 M 965 RKJ to LIB 1066 14/2/02 back to M965 RKJ on 13/11/06. (LIB sold on retention1/07)
58 J430 WFA to KIW 1066 on 8/5/02 to DIG 6213 on 9/06 with sale of vehicle.
60 M351 TDO to BHZ 1066 on 25/2/03 then WIL 1066 on 14/10/03 (BHZ1066 sold on retention)
61 K297 UKR to OIL 1066 on 12/6/03
62 D352 CBC to GIL 1684 in 4/90, D410 OSJ in 12/91, HBZ 4673 in 1/93, JAZ 1066 on 8/10/03 then D785 GCD on 8/10/04
63 N183 WMS to UG 1066 on 14/7/04 back to N183 WMS on 8/3/06
64 R46 JUB to JIL 1066 on 3/8/04, UG 1066 on 17/5/07, to R760NUF on 28/04/09
65 T361 AFG to FAZ 1066 on 7/10/04
66 L317 YDU to JAZ 1066 on 3/3/05 (Fleet No. 66 sold as DIG 3765. Transfer as 29/5/07)
67 P639 ROU to PAZ 1066 on 33/8/05 back to P639ROU in 2/09.
68 R128 AWF to CAZ 1066 on 18/7/05
69 ER 75 AA to GAZ 1066 on 15/11/05 to M496 XJK on 23/10/07
70 N36 PDF to OIL 1066 on 21/2/06 (OIL 1066 latterly sold on retention)
71 YR02 YTH to WIL1066 on 19/1/07 back to YR02 YTH on 21/11/07
72 YR02 YTG to JIL 1066 on 17/5/07 back to YR02 YTG on 21/11/07
73 T713 YDV to JAZ 1066 on 29/5/07 back to T713 YDV in 7/08
74 T174 BVV to JIL 1066 on 30/1/08
75 V403 BNH to WIL 1066 on 30/1/08
77 V7 PCC to GAZ 1066 on 28/4/08
78 V74 GKH to KLZ 1066 on 13/5/08 back to V74 GKH on 22/09/09
79 WV51 ZZG to MNZ 1066 on 28/08/08
80 R16 CTC to FX51 BOH on 17/11/08, to JAZ 1066 on 4/12/08
81 Y373 OFE to PAZ 1066 on 01/04/09
82 S 577 ACT to UG 1066 on 28/04/09
83 T243 MHK to KLZ 1066 on 22/09/09, sold on vehicle 30/10/09

Appendix V: Photographic Record of the Fleet

FIG

54	*DY 5849 Dennis GL, in the early 1930s at Caroline Place Stand. Driver's identity unknown.*
55	*CKF 783, Bedford WTB with C26R Wilmott body,at Hellingly Hospital on visitors' excursion, late 1950s.*
56	*EDY 44, Bedford OB with C29F Plaxton body, at Breeds Place Stand (opposite St. Mary-in-the Castle) in July 1971.*
57	*BEN 301, Bedford SB3 with C35F Duple body, at Breeds Place Stand in July 1971.*
58	*EJK 350, Bedford SB3 with C41F Duple body, at Piltdown in 1971.*
59	*6666 AH, Bedford SB1 with C41F Duple body, at Breeds Place Stand in the early 1970s.*
60	*XBK 576, Bedford SB5 with C41F Duple body, location unknown.*
61	*GPC 58C, Bedford VAL with C52F Plaxton body, at Breeds Place Stand in the mid-1970s.*
62	*NDK 653G, Ford Transit 12-seater minibus, at Breeds Place Stand c1975.*
63	*DHN 455C, Bedford VAS1 with Plaxton C33F body, outside Githa Road Depot after a wash-down.*
64	*MPE 777P, Bedford CF 12-seater minibus by Robin Hood; body builder's official photo at their works.*
65	*KRL 905L, Bedford NJM with C41F body, in London at Hyde Park Corner on a private hire.*
66	*RDY 512S, Ford Transit 12-seater with Williams Deansgate minibus body, in Githa Road when new in 1977.*
67	*RPM 407G, Ford Transit 12-seater minibus, outside All Saints School, Githa Road.*
68	*KNK 357G, Bedford VAS5 with C29F Duple body, at Epsom Racecourse on "Derby Day".*
69	*VAL 965L, Bedford YRT with C53F Plaxton body, at St. Margarets Road Depot.*
70	*AKT 949V, Bedford CF Dormobile C16F, at Githa Road Depot in 1984.*
71	*RLR 28L, Bedford PJK with C29F Plaxton body, in Githa Road in 1982.*
72	*TJK 616S, Bedford HA van, at Githa Road in 1988.*
73	*ODJ 52R, Bedford NJM with C41F Plaxton body, in Bedford Road in 1984.*
74	*JHC 178Y, Bedford PJK with C29F Duple body, in Githa Road Depot in 1983.*
75	*B175 LMY, Ford Transit Mellor C16F, at Dover Hoverport on 7 July 1991.*
76	*JEC 407T, Ford Transit Dormobile C16F, in Githa Road in October 1986.*
77	*MCD 795W, Ford Transit Dormobile C14F, in Githa Road Depot in August 1985.*
78	*URO 921E, Bedford VAM with C45F Plaxton body, in St. Margarets Road Depot in June 1986.*
79	*JRM 800L, Bedford PJK with C29F Duple body, at St. Margarets Terrace in October 1986.*
80	*MAX 331X, Bedford PJK with C29F Plaxton body, in Githa Road 12 April 1987.*
81	*D713 HUA, Freight Rover with B16F Optare body, at Warrior Square bus stop on 5 May 1993 on service EC1 (the first commercial service) operating from Ponswood Industrial Estate to Ore Kings Head.*
82	*GDY 124X, Honda Acty Pickup, at St. Margarets Road Depot in August 1988.*
83	*NKM 133, Leyland Leopard with C53F Plaxton body, at Claverham School in June 1992. This coach was subsequently purchased by Stephen Dine as a separate enterprise from 1995 to 1997, operating as "Acclaim Travel"*
84	*200 FXM, Ford Transit Dormobile C16F, at Warrior Square in August 1989.*
85	*JLN 237N, Bristol LHS with C35F Plaxton body, at the West Hill Centre in November 1989.*
86	*H389 KPY, CVE Omni C21F, at Fairlight Country Park in September 1990.*
87	*H390 KPY, the second CVE Omni, at Western Docks, Dover in May 1991.*
88	*A843 XFW, with transferred number plate 200 XFM, Bedford YMP with C41F Plaxton body, at Babbacombe, Devon in March 1993.*
89	*B157 FWJ, Bedford PJK with C27F Plaxton body, at Mayfield College in August 1994.*
90	*F486 XON, Freight Rover Carlyle C16F (right) and J397 KOR, Renault Master Jubilee C15F, at Summerfields Sports Centre in November 1993.*
91	*FIL 8605, Bedford YMP with C38F Plaxton body, at Battle in December 1995.*
92	*IIL 6765, Ford with C53F Plaxton body, by St. Margarets Terrace opposite the Depot, in July 1995.*
93	*J996 MKM, OBC Omni B20F, at Dudley Road in January 1996.*
94	*CBM 12X, Leyland Tiger with C53F Plaxton body, at Broomham School, Guestling in February 1998 during Jan Auer's ownership.*
95	*F572 HUF and H165 OHK, both Ford Transit C14F, at Broomham School, Guestling in 1998 during Jan Auer's ownership.*

FIG
96 K885 BRW, Toyota Optimo with C21F Caetano body, at Tenterden in August 1999 during Jan Auer's ownership.
97 LIL 9292, DAF with C53F Plaxton body, at St. Margarets Road Depot in August 1999 during Jan Auer's ownership.
98 L760 SDY, Ford Transit Dormobile C20F, on Westminster Bridge in May 2000, after Stephen Dine's take-over of Empress Coaches Ltd.
99 EBM 460T, Bedford YMT with C53F Plaxton body, in St. Margarets Road, May 2000.
100 E768 HCD, with transferred number plate JAZ 1066 (the first of many "cherished" 1066 plates); Ford Transit Dormobile DP20F, on the evening journey of service 303 at The Ridge, Hastings in June 2000.
101 DBB 127V, with transferred number plate BHZ 1066, Bedford YLQ with C35F Plaxton body, at Worth Abbey in June 2001.
102 DBB 127V, Bedford YLQ with C35F Plaxton body, in St. Margarets Road; rear view showing the owner's name as "Stephen Dine and Son" after the arrival of Joshua.
103 D77 HRU (JAZ 1066), Bedford YNT with C53F Plaxton body, at Dover East Cliff in July 2001.
104 L408 ORC (KIW 1066), Iveco C19F at Winchelsea, August 2001.
105 D36 ALR (BHZ 1066), Bedford YMP Plaxton C41F, at Hastings Old Town in August 2001 with the "Battle of Hastings" livery.
106 M965 RKJ (LIB 1066), Ford Transit Devon DP16F, at Conquest Hospital on service 346.
107 J430 WFA (KIW 1066), Mercedes-Benz Plaxton C25F, at Bybrook, Ashford, now repainted out of the Golden Jubilee livery (compare Fig.44).
108 NEC 237K Bedford VAL Plaxton C53F, at Buckswood School, 13 February 2003.
109 M351 TDO (BHZ 1066) Mercedes-Benz Autobus Classique C33F at Bexhill Station, in June 2003.
110 K297 UKR (OIL 1066) OBC Omni DP20F opposite Depot, in October 2003.
111 HBZ 4673 (JAZ 1066) Mercedes-Benz Integral C53F, at Lathe Barn, Burmarsh in July 2004.
112 N183 WMS (UG 1066) Ford Transit Tourneo 8 seater, at Paradise Park, Newhaven in July 2004.
113 R46 JUB (JIL 1066) Ford Transit Devco DP16F, at Lydd in July 2005.
114 T361 AFG (FAZ 1066) Ford Transit C16F, with baggage trailer, at Horntye Park Sports Centre, Hastings in May 2009.
115 L317 YDU (JAZ 1066) Mercedes-Benz Alexander C25F, at De La Warr Pavilion, Bexhill in July 2006.
116 P639 ROU (PAZ 1066) Iveco Bedwas DP25F, opposite Depot in November 2005.
117 R128 AWF (CAZ 1066) Mercedes-Benz DP16F at Bexhill, July 2006.
118 ER 75 AA (ex-RAF) re-registered GAZ 1066, Dennis Javelin Wadham Stringer C41F at Sea Road, St. Leonards-on-Sea in September 2005.
119 N36 PDF (OIL 1066) Iveco Bedwas DP24F, in Boyne Road, Hastings in December 2007.
120 YR02 YTH (WIL 1066) Optare Alero DP16F, in Gurth Road, Hastings in December 2007.
121 YR03 YTG (JIL 1066) Optare Alero DP16F, in November 2007.
122 T713 YDV (JAZ 1066) Toyota Caetano C26F, in November 2007.
123 T174 BVV (JIL 1066) Ford Transit DP15F at West St Leonards School. July 2009.
124 V403 BNH (WIL 1066) Ford Transit DP15F, at Depot in April 2008.
125 XPT 454F, Bedford CA Utilabus C11F, visiting Rambler Coaches Depot in April 2008.
126 V7 PCC (GAZ 1066) Mercedes-Benz Autobus Nouvelle C29F, in interim livery on 14 December 2008.
127 V74 GKH with replacement vehicleT243 MHK (KLZ 1066) at depot 22/10/09.
128 WV51 ZZG, Citroen Despatch (special conversion) 2 seater (non-PCV) at depot June 2009.
129 R16 CTC (JAZ 1066) Mercedes-Benz Optare C16F, (on right) with PAZ 1066, April 2009.
130 Y797 OFE (PAZ 1066) Mercedes-Benz Optare C16F at Chatham Dockyard (re-registered to PAZ 1066) July 2009.
131 S577 ACT (UG 1066) Mercedes-Benz Autobus Nouvelle C29F, at Fort Newhaven September 2009.

54

55

56

57

58

59

60

61

62

63

64

65

66

67

68

69

70

71

72

73

74

75

76

77

78

79

80

81

82

83

84

85

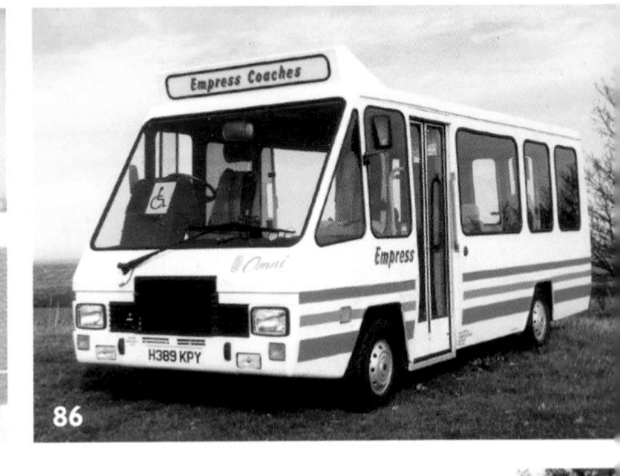

86

87

88

89

90

91

92

93

94

95

96

97

98

99

100

101

102

103

104

105

106

107

108

109

110

111

112

113

114

115

116

117

118

119

120

121

122

123

124

125

126

127

128

129

130

131

Phone 162.

EMPRESS SALOON COACHES

16, EDMUND ROAD, HASTINGS.

Trip ....Bodiam.... *Fare* ..2/6.......

Time and Date ..2.30......28 May

C	5	9	13		20
D	4	8	12	16	19
				15	18
1	3	7	11	14	
	2	6	10		17

404

GUY, PRINTER, HASTINGS, TEL. 320.

Private Parties Catered for. Estimates Free.

The Proprietors reserve to themselves the right to alter, suspend or withdraw the running of any vehicle or Trip without previous notice and will not be liable for any loss, damage, injury, or inconvenience caused to any passenger from any of these causes. Money returned if Trip is suspended. We reserve to ourselves the right to cancel any journey when less than 8 persons have booked seats prior to the advertised starting time.

49 Excursion ticket from the 1930s, white paper, in booklets, approx. 4" square, with seating plan of the first coach.

Empress Coaches

Proprietor :

A. W. PATTEN, 1, Magdalen Road, St. Leonards-on-Sea, Sussex.

Phone Hastings 430621

Date............ Trip............

Cash Paid............

Driver	4	8	12	16	20	24	28	32	36	41
	3	7	11	15	19	23	27	31	35	40
										39
2	Door	6	10	14	18	22	26	30	34	38
1		5	9	13	17	21	25	29	33	37

We reserve the right to cancel any Drive through insufficient Booking.

50 Excursion ticket from the early 1970s, blue paper, in booklets, 4¾ x 4", with seating plan for 41 seater Bedford SBs.

Empress Coaches

Proprietor :

A. W. PATTEN, 13, Bedford Road, Hastings

Phone Hastings 430621

Date............ Trip............ Time............

Cash @ £............Adult. £............Child

	4	8	12	16	20	24	28	32	36	40	44	48	52
	3	7	11	15	19	23	27	31	35	39	43	47	51
													53
	2	6	10	14	18	22	26	30	34	38	42	46	50
	1	5	9	13	17	21	25	29	33	37	41	45	49

Finish

Start Pass @ £

@ £

Total .... £............ Total

51 Excursion ticket from c1980, for 53 seater Bedford.

Empress Coaches

(A. W. Patten)

Hastings
430621 or
437162

13 BEDFORD ROAD,
HASTINGS,
EAST SUSSEX.

SERVICE TO HELLINGLY HOSPITAL

EVERY WEDNESDAY, ~~AND THE FIRST SUNDAY ONLY IN ANY MONTH~~

Coach leaves:—

Coach Stand, Breeds Place	1255 hours
Harold Place + Coach Station	1300
Silverhill, Sedlescombe Road South	1310
Sidley Station	1325
To arrive at Amberstone, Park House, and the Main Building at:	1355
The return journey starts at the Main Building at:	1600
to be at:—	
Sidley Station	1630
Silverhill	1645
Harold Place	1655

The return fare from Hastings is ~~30p~~ 4.35 and from Sidley ~~25p~~ 4.00

Timetable for Hellingly Hospital Service, April 1975. (Tony Patten)

Empress Coaches

(A. W. Patten)

Hastings
430621 or
437 162

I MAGDALEN ROAD,
ST. LEONARDS-ON-SEA,
SUSSEX, TN37 6EG.

Dear Sir/Madam,

I am pleased to inform you that I can now offer you a Coach to suit the size of your party.

My fleet of coaches consists of a 12-Seater for small groups or a 52-Seater for large groups together with the existing 41-Seaters which are still the most popular size.

Should you need a quotation for an intended outing I shall be happy to submit one without any obligation on your part.

I remain,
Yours faithfully,
A. W. Patten
for Empress Coaches

Mail shot, c1973. (Tony Patten)

Steve, Jayne, Joshua and Bethany. October 2009

Dedicated to Jayne, Joshua and Bethany
for their patience and support while the book was being compiled.